ADVANCED PSYCHIC TECHNIQUES

PAUL FENTON-SMITH

ADVANCED PSYCHIC TECHNIQUES

A Path to Intuitive Mastery

BLUE ANGEL®
PUBLISHING

ADVANCED PSYCHIC TECHNIQUES
A Path to Intuitive Mastery

Published by Blue Angel Publishing®
10 Trafford Court, Wheelers Hill,
Victoria, Australia 3150
Email: info@blueangelonline.com
Website: www.blueangelonline.com

Edited by Cathy Jonas, Peter Loupelis and Cherise Asmah

Cover illustration by Daniel B. Holeman

Blue Angel is a registered trademark of
Blue Angel Gallery Pty Ltd.

ISBN: 978-1-922574-36-7

FSC
www.fsc.org
MIX
Paper | Supporting responsible forestry
FSC™ C007683

Printed on sustainably sourced paper, with soy-based ink.

Dedicated to Alexander.

With thanks to my editor Cathy Jonas
for her skills and patience
and to Melinda for her support.

TABLE OF CONTENTS

The names of people used in examples have been changed, along with other details to protect their identities. In some examples, the people described are composites of several people who have similar experiences.

1. A BAPTISM OF FIRE

IN THE MID-1980S, I HIRED A STALL AS A PSYCHIC READER AT AN annual four-day alternative festival interstate. Three of us drove down to Melbourne, an exhausting nine-hour journey, in an old VW Kombi van. After a brief sleep in a noisy hotel, we scrambled out the door on a frosty morning with a map to the venue. Arriving early, we located our stall space and set up three small reading tables with cloths, inside a cavernous hall, before making some hand-drawn signs.

More experienced vendors wheeled stock in on handcarts, unpacking methodically, while rugged up against the wind that whipped through the hall's open roller doors. Yawning stallholders trudged past with an array of books, posters, crystals and incense burners before the 10 am start time. Thankfully, the café was open and the smell of coffee and fresh bread permeated the hall.

Alice scattered a few small quartz crystals beside her tarot deck, while Javier carefully positioned a huge bottle of water on the floor beside his chair and a small clock on his table, and then settled into his folding chair. I placed an appointment pad, a large magnifying glass, a clear plastic rule and some felt-tipped pens beside my tarot deck and business cards, before getting my reading lamp tested for use by the venue organiser.

When the doors opened to the public, the atmosphere changed immediately. It suddenly felt like a busy airport as the once-empty aisles rapidly filled with eager clients. There was a buzz in the room — a mixture of anticipation, curiosity, impatience in the queues and constant conversation. Visitors pushed through the throng, clutching bags of candles, CDs, books and brochures in every shape and colour imaginable. I couldn't always see the candles but their pungent scents announced their presence. While taking a short break at 1 pm, it took six minutes to reach the hall exit as I fought my way through the heaving crowd. I read for 68 people in four days, talking constantly while leaning forward to be close to the ears of each client. It nearly killed me. (I needed a full-body massage and several visits to an osteopath to correct my posture after returning home to Sydney.) I lost my voice twice on the first day, from trying to speak up over the constant noise of a nearby CD stall that played wailing music that was meant to be relaxing. It cured me permanently from ever wanting a music synthesiser.

The following morning, I arrived armed with lozenges for my throat and handed a packet to Alice and Javier, as they'd be talking as much as I expected to that day. Alice produced a large piece of white paper and listed our names, our fees and the services we provided. To help people identify us, she drew my magnifying glass next to my name, crystals next to hers and Javier's small alarm clock next to his. It was a simple, ingenious solution to help visitors identify us and book directly. Javier was strict about not going over time when working at markets or festivals, so he always kept a small clock on the table. He explained that it also helped remind clients about the time constraints. I've kept a clock in my reading room that's visible to clients ever since.

On Saturday evening, after the festival concluded for the day, the three of us sat in silence at a table in a busy Thai restaurant. Fellow diners were clearing their plates around us and quaffing wine, but even the strong scents of curries and spicy soups weren't enough to arouse our interest in eating. I yawned while toying with the brilliant-white damask table cloth, realising that it would soon be covered in rice, noodles and various sauces. We'd forgotten what we had ordered by the time the food eventually arrived, but it was a welcome restorative. We were exhausted and would have been asleep in the hotel already, except we knew we had to eat to have the strength do it all again the following day. My voice was a barely audible whisper and Alice was silent as she tallied up her readings total for the day. Javier stared off into the distance over my shoulder, blinking slowly like an overtired five-year-old who wants to stay up late to see Santa.

When the waiter arrived at the table, I momentarily forgot where I was and enquired about his sister's health and how his plans for his own business were progressing. Alice laughed at me. "You don't stop do you?" she declared, shaking her head. It occurred to me that I was still in tarot-reading mode — I hadn't switched off before I left the venue. When working with energy, it's important to close down at the end of each day. Remaining open is like leaving the doors and windows of your home wide open to the elements, which can be dangerous. In my case, it meant I was psychically open to absorbing all the energies of the diners in the restaurant that night.

Disconnecting from each client after a session is important to ensure past readings don't influence new sessions. It's also vital to switch off when leaving the reading room and at the end of each day. Without closing down and ensuring proper spiritual cleansing, there is a risk of remaining energetically exposed and vulnerable to collecting negativity. When this happens, people become fuzzy-headed, tired and lack mental focus. Since that festival, I've become vigilant about employing effective methods to energetically close down. I've also made it a point to remind myself that psychic readings are my work, not my life. These days, I consciously close down at the end of each day. This means resisting the temptation to activate my intuition when curious about strangers at another table in a café, about a patient in a passing ambulance, or with friends who are struggling with personal issues. It's like resisting the temptation to click on a link in an email that might contain a computer virus. Idle curiosity could result in unwanted negative outcomes. Not closing yourself down allows you to be energetically drained, resulting in days or weeks of fuzzy thinking and poor decisions.

On the long, monotonous drive home, I pondered aloud, "If the benefit of doing is learning, what's the result of overdoing?"

"Yawning," replied Javier, adjusting his head pillow.

This advanced book is designed for people who are familiar with psychic development basics, such as meditation, being attentive to your physical body, knowing the difference between animal and spiritual intuition and keeping an intuitive diary to monitor personal progress.

MOMENTS OF NOURISHMENT AND JOY

On the path to ongoing internal peace and calm are unexpected moments of absolute joy. These arrive without planning and can make us feel excited to be alive. For Tom, this occurs occasionally when he's surfing. During a gentle calm, an enormous swell suddenly lifts the board beneath him like a rapid elevator, before he descends a wave, swiftly gliding down a shimmering tunnel of turbulent water as he races towards the beach. It's a delicate balancing act but when he's on form, he feels the exhilaration of flying, until the board slips out from under him and he plunges beneath the foamy surface.

For Clarice, joy sometimes occurs on late summer evenings, when she's singing with her band on an evening cruise on Sydney Harbour. The twinkling lights of the Harbour Bridge and the brightly lit sails of the Opera House make an exquisite backdrop for leisurely harbour traffic. The array of illuminations along the coast glow like fairy lights as the vessel turns, revealing a fresh vista. She's helping to create vivid memories for tourists and locals alike, as they sip champagne or dance slowly beneath the gentle glow of a full moon. Some warm summer nights, people on surrounding vessels raise their glasses and smile as her boat slips past.

For me, it occurs when, as a guest speaker, I'm demonstrating tracing psychic cords with volunteers from the audience. Gazing out across a packed room, I see everyone leaning in with excitement and anticipation as they watch the volunteer's face carefully, hoping to be chosen next. Sometimes I have fun with the process.

In one demonstration, Jennie, an active woman in her fifties, walked onto the stage. The room fell silent in anticipation. I immediately intuitively saw a strong energy cord attached to her. I traced it out to see the person at the other end and described him.

"I see you still connected to a man in his late fifties to early sixties. He's short to medium height, fit for his age and beginning to grey around the temples." She shook her head, unable to recognise him. I continued to describe him.

"His hair is dark brown, curly and he has olive skin. He has a strong jaw and I see two thin creases down the cheeks — smile lines."

"No," she said. "I don't know anyone like that." It was time to provide some bold brushstrokes, so I continued.

"He's cheeky, self-motivated and can be stubborn. Think passionate Italian greengrocer." As she shook her head, a young woman called out from the third row.

"Mum! That sounds like dad."

The crowd erupted with laughter as Jennie explained. "That's my ex-husband. We were married for 25 years. I've been trying to forget him." In the mood of the moment, I turned to the group.

"Please give Jennie a round of applause for successfully forgetting her ex-husband." They responded with thunderous applause.

Terry's moment of joy began with a stressful shock. While studying at university, he received an email from the office of the University Dean, alerting him that he was on the Dean's list for the year. Panicked, he assumed it was a register of offenders. He warily scanned his memory, wondering what he might have done to arouse the ire of the Dean. He didn't tell anyone, anxiously wrestling with debilitating thoughts of not being allowed to complete his course.

A few weeks later a large envelope arrived in the mail, displaying the university logo. He was immediately filled with dread. At first, he resisted opening it, fearing expulsion from his course. He anxiously thrust it into a drawer. Pondering what he'd done wrong, Terry devoured an entire family-sized block of chocolate to console himself. What would he tell everyone? How could he not notice that he'd broken the rules? Had the assignment scanning software determined that he'd plagiarised someone's work? Would he be granted a chance to defend himself? Was this notice of student termination?

He had to see for himself. Even bad news is better than not knowing. He abruptly tore open the envelope to discover that he had been selected as the most improved student of his cohort for the year. From despair to elation, he burst into tears with sheer relief. It was such positive recognition for his industrious efforts. With an enormous weight lifted from him, Terry felt seen and acknowledged by his tutors.

Suddenly, the skies above were clear and the demanding written assignments didn't seem so difficult.

By regularly practising the techniques in this book, surprising moments of joy are likely to occur more frequently, even during routine activities. This is due to an increased awareness of abundant opportunities, plus strengthening personal resilience with life goals that require patience and persistence. It reveals how to elevate your gaze from everyday, mundane demands to glimpse your rightful place in the universe.

Building on my previous titles, *Intuition* and *Activate Your Psychic Ability*, this book focuses on strengthening intuitive connections, animal scanning and communication. It also includes the enormous power of spiritual nourishment for a more rewarding, deeply meaningful life. A worthwhile, motivated life makes the pursuit of difficult goals easier, especially with the awareness that achieving them is part of your deeper purpose.

Advanced Psychic Techniques explores the role of spiritual masters, finding inner light in dark times, using intuition to identify personal opportunities and dealing with urgent distractions from deeper, life purpose. Simple daily habits to improve individual perception are included, along with how to maintain vital soul sustenance throughout life. Suggestions for moving beyond simple divination to actively pursuing your unique spiritual path are also considered. Mastering these straightforward techniques can change your life forever.

Are you ready for the next step?

2. ADVANCED INTUITIVE METHODS

WE WERE BORN TO BE CREATIVE, RESOURCEFUL AND INTUITIVE beings. This book is a map to reclaiming your divine right by improving internal perception and restoring vibrant inner spiritual light. Developing better judgement when making choices and more easily identifying your unique path in life are some of the benefits.

People who are more experienced with intuitive development usually realise that it's not something to do from time to time, like an occasional yoga class or an impromptu stroll through nature. For individuals in professional practice, regular meditation, personal spiritual cleansing, pursuit of spiritual nourishment and avoidance of recreational drugs and alcohol are all part of what makes spiritual growth attainable. These are essential foundations they rely on when giving psychic readings to friends and strangers because these activities can severely deplete personal energy reserves.

For professional psychics, time spent each week in consultations are supported by a range of positive habits to ensure that they are centred, focused and spiritually replenished between clients. People who consult them pay a fee for the time together in a session and the years spent honing and refining their skills. This includes sharpening their information retrieval methods and their expertise at presenting information so that it's well received and more easily processed.

Many years ago, I worked alongside a psychic who had become bitter with life, especially her relationship. She triumphantly announced how long each client's relationship would last. This spiteful approach overlooked the client's history, emotional burdens, childhood role models or personal self-esteem. Instead of encouraging people to explore relationship options or accounting for each client's past, she bluntly announced her bad news. For her, consultations were simply a way to spread misery. Between clients, she sat slumped in despair and frustration at being unable to change her wretched relationship, while shrouded in stale cigarette fumes from her partner's serious smoking habit. She lacked effective methods for personal nourishment, probably feeling powerless to shape her own life. Experienced professional psychics are usually skilled at glimpsing existence from the client's perspective as well as maintaining an independent view.

Personal spiritual development and psychic hygiene are the equivalent of training for a marathon. They are essential at the beginning of a reading, to discover if the water suddenly becomes very deep and cold. This occurred several years ago for me during a pure clairvoyance reading with a woman in her fifties. Katrina enquired about someone who had passed away, only giving a first name, Jo. Her carefully framed question revealed nothing of her relationship with the deceased. Instead, it was asked without a trace of emotion, as though she was asking a spare question to take up the final minutes of the session.

I assumed that she was a former partner or perhaps a relative and was utterly surprised when a young woman stepped forward into view. Her solemn expression hinted at the heavy burden from her recent life.

"I guess I owe her an apology," she began. I immediately felt an overwhelming sense of regret and knew instantly that she'd taken her own life.

"Did Jo take her own life?" I probed gently. She nodded, suddenly holding back tears.

"She seems to be in her early twenties. Was this the age she died or was she older?" Previously I've seen people who died in old age but didn't enjoy their final years. Consequently, when they reach the other side, they revert to a favourite age, when life seemed full of promise and they felt more alive to possibilities.

This can be confusing, especially if I describe a person's mother at age 27 when the client is already 53 and cannot recognise her parent from my description. She might not have even been born until her mother was 38, so it's often only when I begin to provide additional information about that deceased individual that clients recognise them.

Jo explained that she had to stop her own inner pain and that seemed like the best way at the time. She had no idea that it would immediately derail her mother's life, end her marriage and cast a long shadow over her remaining years. I enquired how she was now and she explained that she had learned to be patient. Sometimes when people end their own lives, they don't cross over to the other side immediately. They have to wait until the time when they were due to pass over and then they are free to move forward. Jo explained that she still had eight years to go.

I intuitively scanned back through her life to discover the searing pain that catapulted her towards her untimely end. A predatory male teacher had trashed Jo's boundaries when she was aged 12, sexually molesting her. It occurred continuously for around nine months. Jo felt powerless to stop the man's abusive advances. Jo explained that she wanted to fall asleep to forget what she felt inside. When I relayed this description to Katrina, she sighed, explaining that she'd used sleeping tablets to end her life.

Rarely do personal readings become so intense but when they do, it's vital that the reader is aware of how much information can be safely revealed to the client. This sensitive information might include the particular underlying spiritual lesson for the client in these events. If it is not something a psychic might say aloud, the reader can incur karma for influencing the person's life direction. It's essential to remember that what is being intuitively glimpsed or sensed is not the whole picture — just what can be currently seen.

Being intuitive is about being conscious. To be aware, it's important to temporarily put aside personal burdens, to carefully observe another person's life. Tread lightly because it involves stepping into another individual's dreams, hopes and aspirations by immersing yourself in their fears, regrets and unresolved issues. When connecting energetically, be careful to leave no footprints. Remember that although invited in, it's only for the duration of the reading. When ending this connection as the session concludes, it's a reader's responsibility to detach from clients, ensuring that no psychic energy cords remain. For more information on cutting psychic cords see my book *A Secret Door to the Universe* (Academy Publishing 2017).

Don't simply imagine that these cords to clients are dissolving. That's no more effective than wishing you went to the gym every day for a year while sitting on a comfy sofa, sipping tea and scoffing cupcakes. Dreaming isn't doing. Imagining is only the first step.

In basic intuitive development courses, I request volunteers in the class to test their psychic defence shields. When they are protected or closed to the outside world, I locate a strong energy cord they have to a partner, a parent or a child and use this as a freeway through their protection. I feel like a burglar when doing this but it's essential to demonstrate how easy it is to bypass inadequate psychic protection. From the moment a volunteer declares that he or she is secure, it only takes about three seconds to begin describing the individual's health and tightness in the neck and shoulders and to detail family members. I end each demonstration with these questions.

- Am I inside your protection?
- How long did it take to safeguard yourself?
- How long did entry take after you declared you were secure?

When working in this area professionally, it's important to not simply understand psychic cords but to be able to see them. Some readers need to be in meditation to glimpse these energy threads, to ensure that they're not imagining them. In psychic readings, these are valuable links to people around clients or burdensome ties, restrictively binding them to former partners and past friends. The psychic reading process can involve forming energetic connections to those people too, so it's essential to disconnect any cords formed during the session. Regular personal spiritual cleansing is vital.

When you can see them, it's important to locate personal threads, to periodically sever those to people who are no longer in your life. Then, with practice, it's possible to trace personal ties out to those parts of yourself that might have been left behind, because of trauma or past pain. By retrieving these energy bodies, a person becomes increasingly present and more effective in the moment. It's like marshalling a competent battalion with shared goals and aims. This can be done gradually, increasing personal energy reserves and awareness of opportunities for joy in everyday life with each new part recovered.

Finally, it's possible to identify two essential energy tunnels for personal spiritual development. One is to a living master and the other to an ascended spiritual master. The first is someone alive today somewhere in the world who is responsible for the spiritual advancement of a group of people. Most people never personally encounter these individuals but are likely to connect with them during sleep at night, when spirit bodies freely explore while the physical body rests.

Ascended spiritual masters have previously passed through the world and are known for their advanced understanding of life and the universe. If, for example, a person's living guide is a Buddhist monk in Thailand or Tibet, it's likely that his or her ascended master is the original Buddha. One advanced teacher is responsible for guiding an individual's spiritual development during this life and the other guides their spirit after death. The work a person does in this life towards soul nourishment is practice for a spiritual journey beyond this life. It's a long voyage that requires adequate preparation.

Nourishing the soul includes regular meditation, prayer, appreciating time alone in nature, yoga, daily periods set aside for reflection and gratitude, creative endeavours and reading spiritually uplifting books. These are all methods for remembering life's deeper purpose — spiritual growth. Taking time to be with like-minded people can help establish bonds with fellow pilgrims on the path.

When reading for strangers, ask the client's current age and begin with past incidents to gauge accuracy. If the person is 36, work backwards from that age, year by year, pausing when an event appears in the mind's eye. If this process is unfamiliar, practise with volunteers or with current clients. Initially, there is pressure to speak. Consequently, beginners tend to skip over many years until a significant milestone emerges. To prevent undue haste, explain to the client that a minute or two of silence is required to quietly scan backwards. This reduces any compulsion to speak immediately.

In private psychic development lessons, I sometimes arrange for a volunteer on the phone or screen so the student in my office can practise with a stranger. If it's a phone call, I ensure the student has a head and shoulder photo of their practice client. The volunteer can then either confirm the student's accuracy or state that they cannot recall certain events. This doesn't necessarily indicate that the reader is incorrect about past events, only that the recipient can't remember them at that moment. Sometimes I'm so engrossed in describing intuitive images that I don't notice when a client struggles to make sense of a person or situation. When clients cannot keep up, pause, take a deep breath and gently remind them that they'll have a recording of the session for review later at home. Occasionally, predictions can take decades to eventuate, as the email below reveals.

> *Over a decade ago (maybe fifteen years?) I saw you for a psychic reading. You were convinced you saw me buying an old house — small windows, dark, cool. I thought NO WAY. It's the complete opposite to what I would buy. I put it out of my mind. A few years after that we chatted on the phone and after enquiring how I was you asked me if I ever bought that house. I said NO WAY. I put it out of my mind. On Friday we exchanged contracts on a house that is old, dark, cool, with small windows ... I had a lightning bolt moment and it occurred to me that this is possibly what you saw in my future. You were so convinced. I was adamant it couldn't be right ... and now look! So many years later it has come to fruition. I thought I'd let you know. N.W. — Sydney.*

Practising readings with strangers provides opportunities to build skills in an environment students can experience as professional readers. They allow novices to become familiar with natural pauses while intuitively searching for events. Then the conversation resumes to reveal what has been sensed. With experience, the process speeds up. Sometimes I have to slow a student down, as the internal pressure to deliver information makes them rush through descriptions, leaving no time for the client to scan back to recall an incident.

This occurred with a student who was taking lessons in animal scanning. At one point, Ji described the volunteer's dog, a Belgian Shepherd. He mentioned that it could appear fierce, with its thick black fur and piercing dark eyes but was also slightly loopy, becoming especially playful and excited around children.

"I have a Husky," responded the client on screen. "The Belgian Shepherd was my previous dog. Yes, loopy is a good word to describe him around kids." The student looked at me quizzically. Why was he seeing a deceased animal and not her current canine? "Find and trace the cord between them," I suggested. Soon, he was describing her current dog and she was nodding affirmatively. Periodically, I held up a hand-written sign which read "slowly" so that he'd pause long enough for his client to absorb the details.

Next, intuitively scan the person's current circumstances. These are usually the most pressing concerns for clients, so it's important to take some time with this. Then explore future events. Skip ahead, year by year, pausing at significant moments in the future. These might include a baby arriving in the family, a new home, a dream job in a different location or memorable travel with a partner or good friend.

During one of these forward scans in a recent reading, I moved ahead only one year to see my client traversing a pilgrim's walk on the Camino trail in Spain. I became intuitively aware that Kate was completely present when hiking, experiencing each moment of almost every day she pursued her goal. She was more alive to her surroundings than she'd felt in her entire 44 years. Aware of the uneven terrain while attempting to identify a range of foreign languages spoken by fellow hikers, she squinted against the hot sun while appreciating the cool juice from her flask. The dry heat meant that even a slight breeze kept her cool in the blazing sun. Although her feet were tired, her heart was content.

I suggested she take 60 seconds at the end of each day to record a quick video on her phone, describing her experiences that day. Incidents, emotions and personal realisations about our lives are easily forgotten a few days later. Several months after her trek, she emailed to say that she had returned from her expedition in Spain and had recently viewed some of her footage.

"It was amazing. The daily insights into myself and my life were unbelievable. It was like I was giving myself the most startlingly clear assessment of my life I've ever received. I'm going back. I have to do this every year or two from now on, for my sanity. I can't risk sleepwalking through my life again."

Sometimes clients arrive for a reading to explore a current issue that's causing pain. However, when examining that particular matter, a reader might discover it's a symptom of a deeper pattern of behaviour. Careful investigation can agitate unexpected memories and feelings that cannot be resolved during the session. This is why it's essential to suggest that clients go easy on themselves after a personal reading, because intense intuitive scrutiny might stir up a range of troubling or triggering issues.

Intuitive readers may not notice this at the time. Even if they are aware of it, they don't know the circumstances that caused the original disturbance. During a tarot course many years ago, we were in an old wooden building where some of the doors wouldn't stay closed without turning a key in the lock. It was a bleak, wintry day and we were huddled around an inadequate fan heater designed to warm a much smaller space.

While explaining a card's meaning, I casually walked over and pushed the door closed, turning the key to ensure it kept the cold breeze out. From my peripheral vision, I noticed a young woman sitting close to the door promptly clasp her hands while holding her breath. She'd effectively dissociated immediately. I knew that if my actions had triggered her somehow, I needed to remedy this or she wouldn't be present for the rest of the course. I immediately unlocked the door and asked her to place her handbag against it, inviting her to be in charge of the entry for the rest of the course.

The colour returned to her face when I observed her again later. Her reaction indicated that turning the key in a lock might have reminded her of an experience where she wasn't free to leave a situation. If so, excitement about learning the tarot might have become a test of endurance until she could escape.

Becoming more intuitive begins with being aware. To be mindful, it is essential to put aside personal burdens temporarily, to carefully observe another individual's life without judgement. This is what psychics do when giving readings to other people. Remember that the clairvoyant's role is one of a perceptive guest, briefly given permission to access someone's energy field to notice and tell the story of that person's life.

It's important to resist the urge to rapidly answer pivotal questions around deep issues, especially when presented as afterthoughts or insignificant queries. Some clients leave their core questions until it's announced that the session has concluded. When this happens, be firm with personal boundaries. If the individual doesn't ask an important question early on in the session when invited, that's an issue for a counselling session, not for an intuitive reading. If this client leaves a session disappointed, it reflects individual boundaries and behaviour rather than the reader's skills.

USING THE INTUITIVE ZOOM FEATURE

In a recent tarot reading, Renita asked about a current love relationship. The significant card in the layout was *The Emperor* (reversed). This describes an undisciplined man. I explained that it looked positive and that they were friends as well as partners, a promising start. She agreed with my description of her partner but not that he was undisciplined.

She then asked if it would be a lasting partnership and the cards indicated that it would likely be a short union. When I told her this, her expression flattened and she sighed softly.

"He's the first man I've loved," she explained. It occurred to me that perhaps I was too close and needed to zoom out to glimpse her whole life. In doing this, I flashed forward to her final day in this life to enquire how many significant partners she had pursued during her lifetime. The answer was three. I then needed to know what number Bernardo was.

"How many important relationships have you had so far in life?" I asked her.

"Bernardo is the first."

"What age are you now?"

"Thirty-seven."

"Why do you think you've waited until age 37 to meet a suitable man?" I asked.

"I don't know."

"I think you'll have three significant partners in your life." She looked horrified, so I continued searching further. I scanned ahead year by year before telling her what I had seen.

"At 42 I see you with a small child, a girl. Her father is not Bernardo but you're happy with your current relationship and home life. This little girl has assessed both parents carefully. In her mind, her dad is fun but a bit flaky but her mother is her rock. She knows that if anything happens, you'll find a solution and make life stable again. That relationship will last for decades but you might eventually outlive your husband. In later life, there is another man. You insist that he's just a friend, who lives in a separate house but everyone knows the score when they see you together.

From where you sit today, it's as though a waiter will offer a menu of opportunities, returning to your table two more times. It's your choice to peruse the card or refuse it. From what I've seen today, you won't likely decline these three opportunities."

"Then what do I do about Bernardo? You see, he's married and although they have separated, they still live in the same place."

"I think that within two years, you'll leave your job and your link to Bernardo. When he doesn't step up to be with you, you'll have your answer. Don't be sad that it ended. Instead, be glad that Bernardo provided a chance for love and more rewarding opportunities. One more thing. When I mentioned he was undisciplined, you insisted that that wasn't correct. Would a reliable man live with his wife and date another woman secretly?"

By stepping back intuitively, I was able to jump forward to the end of Renita's life and ask her about relationships. Then I knew what I was looking for — two more men. By focusing on the present and moving forward from age 37, year by year, I could see approximately when these men would likely arrive. It was possible to narrow it down to the actual year, but in Renita's session, we were pressed for time. Being slightly vague about the next man's arrival acknowledged her free will. Personal choice was essential because she would live with the consequences of her decisions. As a reader, it's not my life. I'm only a witness, taking a fleeting glimpse of a stranger's life at a small table beside a tall window, overlooking a leafy garden on a cloudy afternoon.

A SHORTER PATH TO PSYCHIC DEVELOPMENT

Almost anyone can become a natural psychic. Repetitive trauma often forces people to open up intuitively by dissolving personal boundaries but this is not usually a positive way to proceed. Psychics who become intuitive as a result of intense emotional upheaval often have porous boundaries. Their energy fields fill every room they are in, just like small children. These individuals sometimes predict events ahead without invitation, naively trespassing into the energy fields of complete strangers. It becomes an ego trip or a way for them to feel special. Experienced readers and counsellors understand that it's actually a symptom of their own unresolved suffering.

For people who want to consciously improve personal intuition to make better life decisions, it's essential to remember that 'psyche' is another word for 'soul'. When the soul is nourished, personal intuition naturally improves, as it's easier to hear inner guides when the mind is calm and still. Spiritual growth is an essential part of our unique journeys through life. The most effective way to intuitively evolve is to focus on spiritual development. This involves forming positive habits that nourish the soul, such as spending time in nature, regular prayer, meditation or simply sitting still and requesting spiritual light.

Over the past four decades of consulting with personal clients, there has been a group of people who seem to arrive and depart their sessions without any divine light ever reaching them. They find it very difficult to meditate or pray as they are often mentally fuzzy, spiritually hungry and exhausted, often through no fault of their own. It's as though the paths of others are well lit but their own trails are traversed in darkness.

For these people, group meditations can help, even in gatherings as small as two. When individuals adept with deep meditation draw down spiritual light, those close to them also receive some of that soothing energy. When people pray together, it's the same. For extremely stuck individuals, if they unite with a friend who prays aloud on their behalf, spiritual light reaches them. It's a chance for them to experience and remember what they are aiming for in personal meditations. Sometimes these are the only times they experience spiritual radiance, as they begin to improve their own skills in asking and receiving.

Likewise, if they ask aloud for a friend who is present, divine energy enfolds both of them. It's as though people who feel forgotten have their own pleas answered when they appeal on behalf of someone else. This involves accepting that although they might believe they have nothing to offer, they can still request light for someone else. The selfless act often ensures that that same radiance envelops them too.

When feeling very stuck, an effective process is to ask a friend to meditate with you or pray aloud for you while sitting together. This can be done at a distance on the phone or via a video call. If there are specific areas to focus on, bring a list so the support person can be precise about what you need right now. Specific is good when directing light where it's required. If you prefer the meditation path, ask a friend to meditate aloud, so you can hear their request of love and spiritual radiance for you. Listen in silence as someone asks for spiritual light to replenish you.

For people who feel forgotten by the world, God or Buddha, this can be a spiritually significant experience. It's also reassuring to hear someone ask on your behalf, for a healing source of energy that is your spiritual birthright. Done repeatedly, this can be a way to forge new pathways to spiritual nourishment when praying or meditating alone.

In a recent reading, I carefully scanned through a life filled with burdens and obligations as Lorraine nodded silently. She wanted to know when it would be her turn for happiness.

"Will there be anybody special for me in the future? I don't even need a relationship. Just some male company — a friend would be nice." Already in her sixties, I scanned ahead to see her joining a small prayer group. She felt slightly embarrassed at being there but the other members seemed warmly welcoming. After a few months of weekly meetings, another member, Tuarno, asked if she'd be interested in just the two of them praying together once a week at his house. A quiet, thoughtful man, he had prepared a short outline of the process for future meetings and invited Lorraine to add anything she wanted to include in her prayers.

From the very first visit, both of them were bathed in significantly more radiance than they had ever experienced before in their larger group. Time slowed, as they felt blissfully immersed in each moment. Although this was not a love relationship, their weekly shared requests for divine nourishment provided abundant sources of pure energy. It was like a refreshing river of light, cleansing them of their troubles every week for years. After the second meeting, Lorraine was bursting with happiness and wanted to tell her friends about her discovery. Then she immediately worried that they might ridicule her choices or beg to join their weekly meetings and perhaps dilute the joyful experience somehow.

"This is the love that you've been searching for your whole life, only it's not from a man and it's not from this world," I told her. "It's more than you anticipated and can sustain you throughout your final years. It's as though you've found a radiant source of light and you want to tell the world. However, you also wish to take this bountiful secret to your grave. You'll write a journal for yourself, carefully describing how you feel in the hours after each meeting. After you pass over, I see a woman in her late thirties secretly reading passages from it every night. She finds it sustaining and it sparks a quest to find a prayer or meditation partner like you did. It might be your son's wife. She won't relinquish your journal, jealously guarding it and revisiting particular sections over the years."

Lorraine looked at me nervously, asking, "All this is ahead for me?"

"Yes, when you overcome your resistance to group support and join that weekly gathering. The reason why the younger woman loves your journal is because you were still immersed in spiritual light each week while writing it. Your life is like a cake. After the hard work of mixing and baking, it's time to add the icing. This comes last and it's usually the sweetest part."

The shortest path to better intuition and a more sustainable life is to regularly request spiritual radiance, particularly from a personal ascended master, who is simply spiritual light. They are so refined that they only have the shape we give them. Seeing them provides a chance to grasp what is possible for ourselves eventually. However, when receiving this abundant energy, people usually feel safe, calm, peaceful and warm inside. Consider how it would feel to have all your worries, fears, guilt, shame and regret swept away and replaced with luminescent light. You're suddenly as weightless as a feather, drifting peacefully in a gentle breeze on a sunny afternoon.

In prayer or in meditation, it can be beneficial to ask;

- What can I learn from this painful experience?
- What is my role in the current circumstances?
- What decision or action (if any) did I take to end up in this situation?
- What can I change within myself to avoid this recurring?
- What can I contribute that would be meaningful at this time?
- How can I support ______ in their life right now?
- How could I have better responded to those circumstances?
- In my current struggles (financially, with physical or mental health, with love, with my family, etc.) what is the best approach for a suitable outcome?
- What other activities can nourish me spiritually in my life? (Ponder this one often.)

In this way, reflection time is constructively used to address personal issues to grow emotionally, mentally and spiritually. Consequently, with more awareness, you begin to notice when upheavals occur. It's easier to change direction with a broader view. Eventually, intuition guides personal choices so you can naturally avoid drama or conflict.

By consciously and regularly requesting spiritual light, other people tend to gravitate towards you to unconsciously share some of that uplifting, joyful energy. In personal readings, they soak it up. Sometimes if they have attached entities, these will move across to the reader for a stronger source of energy. This means that with increasing spiritual light drawn down, more personal spiritual cleansing is required to remain clear and centred. By cutting corners, there is a risk of becoming mentally fuzzy, then emotionally choked up and finally, physical health issues emerge.

Wanting a fast track to spiritual mastery is accompanied by increased responsibilities. Just as a professional sportsperson undergoes regular training, maintains a healthy diet and avoids poor lifestyle choices, it's necessary to be vigilant about who or what aids your thriving as well as those people and circumstances that deplete personal vitality. The rewards include a deep sense of purpose in life, increasing awareness of the underlying lessons in everyday struggles and a plentiful source of radiant, peaceful light when needed. You're also likely to produce some creative solutions to ongoing issues and thrive in life instead of constantly struggling.

Developing stronger boundaries around individuals you spend time with is essential to maintaining personal energy balance while avoiding becoming exhausted. This can reduce the need to continuously restore vitality after being carelessly drained by people who selfishly syphon off your reserves to support their poor lifestyle choices. It's vital to remember that everyone has access to the same sources of light but only a few make the effort to ask for it and use it wisely.

For some individuals, this journey begins as a simple desire to make better life decisions. It then progresses to discovering that they can assist others to make more meaningful long-term choices. Eventually, it involves realising that in the bigger picture, there are consequences for changing the direction of the lives of others. The karmically safest option is to teach others how to find this universal light and then step back, allowing them to warmly bask in their own luminescence.

Step one: Make better choices. If 50% of personal decisions led towards positive experiences and opportunities, where might you be in ten years?

Step two: Help others to explore more meaningful options. If you could assist friends, family members or strangers to make improved decisions, how could their lives look in ten years?

Step three: By inspiring others towards their most spiritually rewarding paths in life, through teaching them effective skills, how might your soul evolve in the next 100 years?

These three steps are like planting a flower, a tree or a forest. Planting a flower in the shade of a tall tree might limit its chances of thriving. Positioning a young tree in the centre of a forest forces it to compete with established plants for light and nutrients. Planting a forest requires time, patience and persistence to see the results. This is why it's essential to carefully notice your surroundings when setting goals.

I-SENSE EXERCISE FOR TRAINING INTUITION

I've described this simple technique in a previous book but it's worth mentioning again. It takes five minutes and requires a volunteer to practise with. This process favours talkative people, as speaking continuously for five minutes is necessary. During my introductory and advanced psychic development courses, students complete this exercise on each of the three days.

After their first attempt, I hear comments like, "Five minutes seemed so long," and, "The pressure was enormous." You'd think they had just returned from three months on a space station orbiting Earth. These are the same individuals who routinely make a quick call to a friend that lasts 40 minutes. Some of them do all of the talking during that phone conversation. On their third or fourth attempt, when information flows more smoothly, they frequently don't want to stop.

Please note: this is not an exercise in accuracy, so don't invest any time or money in anything mentioned during this process. It's an introduction to a stream-of-consciousness intuitive method, that helps psychics relax their minds and allow for deeper knowledge and awareness to surface.

For people who read professionally, practise with existing clients at the end of sessions. Introduce the process with, "I'm sensing a bit more but I'm not sure about the accuracy of this information. It's a new method I'm trying out. If you have five minutes, I can tell you what I'm aware of, without recording it." Unless the client is late for an international flight, he or she will say 'yes'.

Steps:

Explain how the necessary pauses from time to time are to make sense of a fleeting intuitive image or to allow for intuitive deepening. By strengthening awareness, you move from everyday events to significant themes in the person's life.

Take the clients fingertips in your hands. This is a simple link for kinaesthetic people who work better with touch. Even if you're not a touch-oriented person, afford yourself every available method for receiving information.

Begin by repeatedly saying, "I sense … I sense …" If you don't sense anything, say, "I sense blank, I sense blank."

The goal is to continuously speak for five minutes. What usually occurs is that beginners come up blank for between 10 and 20 seconds and then begin noticing information about themselves. At some point in the process, students switch from identifying personal information to observing details about their clients. Then, if novices encounter momentary doubts, they revert to stating that they sense blank or being aware of themselves again.

With repetition, amateurs begin to notice when they cross over from details about themselves to intuitive information about the client. When each student relaxes, information flows. For clairvoyant types, it's like watching a film. With clairaudient people, it resembles listening to a podcast about a stranger's life. Clairsentient individuals experience their bodies becoming immersed in sensations related to the volunteer's life. They can experience pain in their joints, lethargy resulting from the client's daily medications or anxiety about an upcoming exam that the client is about to take.

This activity involves speaking without thinking, censoring or filtering words. After a student has completed this exercise a dozen times, it's possible to notice when awareness deepens and the process transforms from personal to client information. The time before the crossover shortens with experience, until one day, it begins with the first inward breath.

Gradually, it becomes easy to direct individual attention to areas of interest to the client, such as career, love relationships, travel opportunities or the person's financial future. At that point, the student begins to filter information, so that the client receives relevant guidance clearly presented and delivered in a tactful, positive manner.

Early practice sessions might sound like this:

> "I sense blank … I sense blank."
> "I sense a small black dog. It has a yellow, rubber duck in its mouth."
> "I sense blank."
> "I sense a baby, waking up and crying after a nap in the late afternoon. It's raining softly."
> "I sense blank."
> "I sense that you're worried about your job stability but are afraid to apply for new positions elsewhere. I sense a birthday party for an elderly relative, with a surprise guest who is famous."

This exercise also provides novices experience with saying aloud their own intuitive glimpses. The word 'sense' is deliberate here, encompassing seeing, hearing and feeling. In advanced courses, when the exercise is extended to ten minutes, students forget to say 'sense' and often say, "I see … I feel …" or, "They are telling me that …" This immediately reveals if they are favouring clairvoyance, clairaudience or clairsentience when retrieving information.

During practice sessions, trainees need to spread out to avoid overhearing each other and being influenced. Shy pupils can lose confidence if sitting close to someone naturally talkative and outgoing. Anyone with a booming voice is encouraged to pair off with an exercise partner outside, further away from the group.

I remind students that after practising this exercise 30 times with different friends and strangers, they are already psychic readers. It's the same process I use with tarot clients. As each person shuffles the deck at the beginning of a reading, I silently state, "The issue today is …" and, "The underlying need for my client today is …" It's a variation of the I-sense exercise. I then pay close attention to observe how quickly what I discovered at the beginning emerges during the session.

In a recent reading, I noticed that the issue for my client was loneliness. It didn't surface during the session and I figured that maybe I was wrong, as Tania seemed chatty, enthusiastic and bubbly throughout. I mentioned what I had perceived when the reading concluded. She immediately burst into tears, surprised that someone had seen beneath her sparkling persona. I gently reminded her that a potential partner who appreciates her genuine warmth and soft kindness was coming soon.

3. READING FOR FRIENDS AND STRANGERS

MANY PEOPLE WHO SEEK TO IMPROVE THEIR PERSONAL intuition don't necessarily want to read for strangers. Instead, they hone their instincts to make better individual decisions, land more rewarding jobs and find suitable life partners. These are admirable reasons for intuitive development because it's possible to be happier, more successful and a better parent when you're not pushing against the tide. Finding an absorbing vocation instead of a mundane job is an important discovery. It shapes a purposeful life and helps us find meaningful ways to give back to others.

Some people choose a different path. They want to help individuals directly through predictions, identifying blockages to happiness or clarifying past incidents that have left emotional scars.

There are countless ways to support others to live more rewarding lives. When reading for David, I noticed that he constantly strove for perfection, impressing others with his achievements but often falling below his own stratospheric expectations. In his career as a psychologist, I intuitively saw him running self-development groups for teenagers and later coaching private clients to fulfil their dreams. He frequently felt as though his efforts were wasted, despite helping and inspiring scores of people throughout the decades of his career.

I enquired why he believed it necessary to burn brightly, like a shooting star, gliding across the sky and into the void. He confirmed that's how he often felt, yet he was unable to answer the question, so I looked ahead to the end of his life.

Soon after passing over, David was met by his good friend, Timothy. The intervening years had taken their toll. David appeared gaunt. He was weary from the struggle and seemed relieved that it was over and pleased to see his silver-haired friend, who towered over him. Despite his huge frame, Timothy was softly radiant, beaming with joy at their reunion. They hugged each other and Timothy said, "Turn around for a moment. Notice the effects of all your efforts. You spent your whole life showing people how they are enough, constantly reminding them that they don't need to strive to be more. You also struggled with self-worth, before realising that what you brought to the table was sufficient. Do you see now how you constantly thought that you could do more? Look at how you've changed their lives positively."

In that instant, David noticed his valuable contribution, while scanning back through the events of his recent life. Focusing on the myriad images of people and events, he saw how he had made a difference to the lives of others.

"Now you've earned a rest," Timothy stated softly. For the first time, David glimpsed how the skills he taught his clients had improved their lives, through their careers and their life choices. Consequently, their children enjoyed better circumstances and their grandchildren too. The positive ripples of David's life of service had improved the existence of people he'd never even met.

In that moment, he was overwhelmed, humbled that his tireless efforts were not wasted. He sobbed at how often he had doubted himself. Timothy slipped an arm around his shoulder and softly asked, "Do you still think that you could have done more?" As I told David what I was intuitively seeing, he became choked up. Tears streamed down my cheeks and I was only a witness. David might forget being told that his persistent efforts were not wasted, but better to have heard it at age 32 than wait until he'd left this life behind.

Reading for strangers is like being invited briefly into their lives as a guest. Clairvoyants need to tread lightly when in the energy of others, to avoid influencing fate. If the person is about to make another poor decision in a long line of imperfect choices, it's better to see how their compass has been skewed than to lecture them about the consequences of their intended actions. If I'm tempted to admonish a client for a wayward decision, I remember some of my own previous feckless pursuits.

Reading for strangers is only one avenue to serving others. There are many equally effective ways to contribute, because purpose in life is often found in what we give back to society. Harry had been retired for ten years and lived with his wife, Helen. They shared a small home in a poor neighbourhood, but it was theirs. He enjoyed sitting on the tiny porch, gazing at his minute front garden. One morning, a group of enthusiastic young children who were playing across his driveway irritated him, shouting and laughing. This had become their weekend routine. They were growing more boisterous in their games, so after a few hours, Harry strode out to move them on.

"Why are you kids always playing on my driveway?" he asked pointedly. They froze.

"There's nowhere else to play," mumbled an older boy.

"Don't you have gardens at home?"

"No."

"What about going to a park?"

"There isn't one around here and we can't walk to the Belmont Park. It's too far." Harry pondered this for a moment. Some of them were too small to tackle a 3 km walk to the park and back.

"I tell you what. If you're here at 8 o'clock tomorrow morning, I'll take you to the park for an hour. Exactly at eight, mind you. Not a minute later. And you have to ask your parents if it's okay," he declared gruffly.

The next morning at 7:50 am, Harry glanced out the window to see four children waiting expectantly on the drive, one clutching a faded ball. He reversed the car out of the garage and they clamoured into the back. These scruffy kids played in the park for an hour while Harry read the paper. He enjoyed the fresh air, the space and having the bench seat to himself while the boys raced across the expanse of grass. He was exhausted from simply watching them and couldn't remember ever having had enough energy to run just for the sake of it. He was surprised how much fun they produced with just a simple ball.

The following Saturday morning, Harry noticed five children waiting eagerly on the drive, so he begrudgingly drove them to the park. Over the next few months, the group expanded to 12 and then 17 kids, three balls and a kite. He enlisted the help of another local, Ken, to ferry locals to the park on weekends. His wife Helen insisted that he count the children before leaving home and again before returning from the park.

Helen eventually made name tags for them to carry in their pockets. The box of tags was left out on the porch at night and the older boys handed them to everyone each Saturday morning before Harry and Ken arrived to collect them. News spread rapidly about the park trips and soon they required more drivers. Even light rain couldn't douse their enthusiasm for an hour of freedom outdoors.

Harry noticed a need in his community and filled it. As the volunteer drivers increased, there were five old guys sitting around together in the park with coffee flasks and sandwiches on weekend mornings. Terry complained about the pain in his hands while Fred stared off into the distance, mulling over his unfinished crossword. As winter approached, they huddled in Ken's car — out of the wind but with a view of the park, to ensure everyone was safe.

"There's a kid out there, running around in a T-shirt and shorts. How is he still alive? It's damn near freezing out there," muttered Tom as he eased himself into the car with a sigh after retrieving his scarf.

"What would you call this outing?" asked Ken on a frosty June morning, clutching a fresh cup of coffee from his thermos.

"It's as if a minibus tour for retirees lost its way in a daycare centre, in a park," quipped Terry.

"Or, it's an example of us staring at what we used to be while they ignore what they'll eventually become," added Tom.

"As we sit here supervising these kids from the sidelines, we're around 80 metres and 70 years apart," summarised Harry. A silence ensued as they contemplated the concept of distance—measured in metres and generations—to the sound of Ken gulping his coffee.

"So, comparing 80 metres and 70 years, which is the greater distance?" enquired Terry.

4. LOST INTUITIVE CONNECTIONS

SOMETIMES DESPITE BEST INTENTIONS, OUR PERSONAL connection to intuitive information falters. During these periods, intuition is fuzzy and a person becomes confused or receives incorrect advice. When uncentred, people can become unaware that they are relying on misleading information for important decisions, which can be disastrous. When using intuitive information for important personal choices, it's best to ask the same questions on several different occasions. If the answers are identical, with additional finer details each time, the information is likely to be accurate.

This repeated process is vital for personal questions as it's more difficult to remain objective when enquiring about your own relationship, job, physical health or your child's wellbeing. When former tarot student, Mai, asked about her career, she was prompted to book a reading because her earlier predictions for herself had not eventuated. Working for her mother's company over the previous two years, she had continuously moved around the organisation whenever she felt restless. She wanted to begin a sales-team project involving overseas expansion. Instead, her current workload was demanding more of her attention and she felt bored and exhausted.

The sales-team plan didn't seem likely. Mai then enquired about a role in the finance department, but she seemed a poor fit for that environment. Instead, she was likely to move to a new city to work for a different organisation. It's possible that when Mai read for herself, she was only asking about her current work environment, so details of a different workplace didn't even surface. Her desire to have a new role that offered a chance to relocate overseas might have influenced how she prepared her questions.

It's difficult to make broad enquiries about your own career after your specific questions have not elicited positive responses. However, an open career query is exactly what might have provided Mai with the information she needed. I suggested that next time she makes personal enquiries and feels dispirited by the responses, she takes a few days or longer to allow her disappointment to subside before exploring the issues more deeply.

If, when testing accuracy, answers to the same questions contradict each other over several days, it's better to examine these issues separately:

- **The motivation for asking these questions.** A strong desire for a specific outcome influences any information received or overlooked. It's not easy to be impartial with yourself, especially when you have to live with the consequences.
- **The process employed to glean information.** By trying different methods (meditation, cutting a tarot deck or dreams at night), it's simple to discover what works best for you.
- **Any potential bias or preconceived ideas that affect the outcome.** Expectation of a particular answer can restrict the inflow of details and even influence how questions are phrased.

There are ways to ensure being centred before another intuitive attempt. If a deadline is approaching, it's essential not to rush or feel pressured to produce an immediate answer. Instead, treat the issue as though someone else asked the question. Emotional distance from the outcome improves your perception and reduces bias. Ensuring clear focus might include a deep meditation to release tension, a brisk walk for a change of scenery, or an hour of yoga or tai chi to restore inner equilibrium. Reading for yourself in the midst of a personal storm is not advised.

Occasionally, past unresolved trauma held in the physical body can override our intuitive impulses. If someone has been through several harrowing job interviews, is experiencing unfair treatment or harassment or is feeling unheard by interviewers, these emotions can surface later, even in a positive interview. When this happens, the body prepares for an onslaught that doesn't actually arrive. This can lead to defensive answers to simple questions and poor performance in a non-threatening situation.

It's important to be aware of this because many natural psychics become intuitive as a result of past trauma. Sometimes a powerful or explosive situation makes it more comfortable for us to have greater awareness of situations and events outside of the physical body instead of within it. This can occur when someone is hyper-alert for danger, such as a child tiptoeing around an unpredictable, explosive parent. This type of unresolved trauma occasionally skews our intuition, forcing us to focus on possible threats while unconsciously overlooking bountiful opportunities. It's a fine line between glimpsing a most likely consequence or dreading an outcome based on past personal experience.

Even in public readings, a psychic might concentrate more on issues, threats and looming trouble than on positive opportunities ahead. A balanced reading usually covers both areas equally. A clairvoyant session that focuses solely on openings can be just as biased and ineffective as a gloomy one because most situations have their strengths, weaknesses, opportunities and threats. To make the most of prospects, it's important to rely on personal talents and experience to overcome individual shortcomings while avoiding potential obstacles. This is a delicate balancing act and is most effective when it finally becomes an unconscious positive habit.

The path to intuitive development is much less painful for people who learn through books, courses, support groups and regular personal practice than through unexpected trauma. It takes longer but leaves fewer scars and there are usually more positive associations and enjoyable discoveries along the way.

Repetitive pressure or trauma can also leave some people with heightened sensitivity to the emotions of others, making it difficult for them to function fully in crowded work environments. Basically, they become burdened by the unexpressed emotions of people in close proximity. Even walking through a busy shopping centre can leave empathetic people feeling exhausted or fuzzy-headed as they are energetically wide open to surrounding energies. Hypersensitive people usually require additional regular spiritual cleansing and psychic protection techniques to ensure clear thinking and emotional balance. Without regular resets, they become fuzzy-headed or more easily distracted from their deeper purpose.

Long-term remedies include working from home or in a harmonious environment. Online shopping is also a bonus for hypersensitive people. If being mentally scattered causes intuitive inaccuracy, look back through the day to become aware of when you were last focused and balanced. Notice, too, what or who uncentred you. It might range from eating sweet foods such as chocolate, a sudden noise, a difficult conversation or receiving an upsetting email. Sometimes a few minutes alone, simply focusing on breathing, can help restore internal balance.

During a recent reading, a bird that was being chased by two others flew directly into my closed office window pane. The sharp bang as it bounced off the glass gave me a shock, and my client looked just as unsettled. The bird stood up and flew away into a tree for safety while I took a moment to breathe deeply and settle myself before proceeding.

Sometimes counselling clients arrive feeling scattered and cannot remember when they last felt a sense of focus and awareness of their personal surroundings. To identify when they were last centred, I ask them what recent situation or experience they last recall clearly. When balanced, most individuals are aware of their surroundings and clearly remember events. When uncentred, it's difficult for them to recall if they have eaten lunch, turned off the lights or made commitments to visit friends.

To minimise the disappointment of waiting for a prediction to eventuate when feeling unbalanced, there are ways to test accuracy during the meditation or intuitive process.

A SIMPLE TEST FOR INTUITIVE ACCURACY

At the end of an intuitive process or meditation, request specific details about the next 48 hours in your life.

Immediately after the intuitive activity, write or record what you saw or heard, including about the next 48 hours. Don't rely on memory; it can be inaccurate.

Two days later, carefully review your notes.

If incorrect, try again, ensuring you're centred before a second attempt.

Try a different intuitive method if you are repeatedly inaccurate. If your first approach was using meditation, you might try dreams at night. One student learned to read the tarot to consult the cards when asking which intuitive methods would work best for her each day. It seemed like an unnecessary additional burden but she believes it fast-tracked her intuitive development.

By using a short-term prediction to test accuracy, it's not necessary to wait up to two years for longer-term predictions to be proven incorrect. You'll also learn not to take inaccuracy personally, while discovering which intuitive techniques work best. No one can be 100 per cent accurate consistently. Every psychic has good runs, interspersed with ordinary moments for many reasons. However, practice and experience usually improve accuracy and consistency.

In a client setting, without the luxury of a 48-hour test, simply go back to past events. Being correct when describing a person's past experiences increases the likelihood of being accurate with future milestones. I use this process in pure clairvoyance readings, where accuracy about the past often gives clients confidence in what I say about future possibilities. They don't always hear it on the day but a recording of the session increases their chances of discovering exactly what was said at a later date.

When Tina asked about marriage, she explained that she was single and felt unlucky in love. In scanning back through her relationship history, I noticed that in her twenties, she had abandoned partnerships with two different men who had wanted to marry her. Passionate, independent and preferring her freedom, she relocated interstate and then overseas, following her career and travel dreams. These were vital goals for Tina but choosing to pursue one objective can sometimes be at the cost of another. She was also subconsciously holding on to a former partner from her late twenties. They had separated but she had not yet released him from her heart to make room for someone new.

When a person is emotionally preoccupied with a previous spouse, new relationships are often with people who also have regrets about their own lost opportunities. It's as though everyone desires a new home but no one wants to clear the land and build solid foundations first.

By tracing back through Tina's past partnerships, I was able to reveal how her actions had led her to where she was, before looking ahead at new possible relationships. I reminded her to release this person, to ensure she'd be ready when a new potential spouse arrived at 36.

"Thirty-six! That's two years away. Who's coming up this year?" she asked pointedly.

"So just to clarify, it's already September and you'd like to meet Mr Right and settle down before Christmas. Is this accurate?" I queried.

"Yes."

"Any travel plans for the rest of this year?" I asked, to underline how she couldn't sit still long enough to build a new relationship. She missed my intention entirely, simply answering the question.

"Just to Hawai'i for a week but that doesn't count," she replied, frowning.

"If your heart is still preoccupied with the man from your twenties when Mr Right does arrive, he won't be able to stay. I challenge you to do the emotional work and not to squander a viable opportunity. It might take every day of those two years. Are you up to the task?"

"Watch me," she declared boldly.

Knowing that Tina couldn't resist a challenge, it was necessary to be forthright to motivate her to change. Her words were focused on meeting a life partner while her actions suggested that this new person might be secondary to travel, adventure and career.

Clouded intuitive communication is caused by a range of different events, including:

- A recent unresolved emotional upset.
- Impatience during the intuitive retrieval process.
- Leaving out some steps in the method.
- Having consumed foods your body is intolerant to.
- Recent consumption of alcohol, medications or recreational drugs.
- Misinterpretation of a dream, if the information is connected to a dream at night.
- Being too attached to a specific outcome. Extreme desire distorts results.
- Reading for a colleague or acquaintance where you don't want to deliver bad news.
- An internal bias about the question, such as a friend asking about having an affair or an intended illegal action.
- Asking the wrong question.
- Surrounding distractions such as a demanding partner, small children, pets or noisy neighbours.

It's not always possible to ensure perfect surroundings for deep, daily meditation, nor to avoid emotional upsets that reduce intuitive accuracy. However, it's easy to try again another day after disappointing results from intuitive attempts.

Don't strive to be brilliant immediately. Occasionally, I see a student who is determined to dazzle others on the first day of a psychic development course. This is the individual who, when learning to ride a bike, wants to sail off with perfect balance on day one, turn a corner and join the Tour de France to finish with a place. It's not realistic. People with unreasonable goals sometimes cut corners to achieve their aims. Skimping on procedures doesn't work and increases the risk of collecting unwanted dross from other people. Shortcuts can become expensive when making spontaneous decisions about a large investment or eloping with someone you've only known briefly. The intuitive process is best not rushed. Take your time or you'll have plenty of opportunities to regret your decisions or actions later. Developing intuitive skills requires patience and persistence but the rewards include a lifetime of better decisions. Confidence is built slowly and steadily.

5. IMPROVING YOUR INTUITIVE CONNECTIONS

SOMETIMES AFTER A RESTFUL NIGHT'S SLEEP AND FOLLOWING a deep, still meditation, it's possible to secure a strong connection to your higher self or guides. When this happens, information flows freely, like fresh, cold water from a mountain stream. The details can be crystal clear, with surprising consequences.

Recently, a client asked during a pure clairvoyance reading why she felt compelled to buy the house she had bought. Kirsten was divorcing her husband several years after moving into the property. Although she felt a powerful urge to buy it from the moment she saw it, they had not been happy together since they moved in.

I intuitively scanned the home, but nothing negative seemed to linger in the building. I then searched the entire property from above, looking into the earth from about ten metres overhead — like a drone's perspective. There was a clear energy line running just beneath the earth's surface diagonally through one corner of the property. It rose from deep down, almost reaching the topsoil before turning back down again like an enormous snake hidden from view. Its path ran beneath one room in the home. On a piece of paper, I drew the view of the property from the street and explained what I had glimpsed.

I asked Kirsten what room was at the front right-hand corner of the building. The house was positioned sideways on the block and the kitchen was in that corner.

"I remember the day I first saw the house with the agent," she explained. "I was standing in that corner of the kitchen when I knew I had to buy the place. It was strange. It was a sense of total conviction that ran through me."

I scanned the energy line again and realised that it amplified emotions and desires. When feeling sad, spending time in that kitchen increases the intensity of that emotion. When angry, the energy running beneath the house was likely to escalate the anger into frenzied rage. When I explained this to Kirsten, she nodded and told me that she was also standing in the kitchen during an intense argument with her husband when she finally made the decision that their marriage was over and he wasn't safe to live with. In a fit of temper her husband hurled some dinner plates at the cupboards next to her and pressed her bodily up against a wall, preventing her from leaving the room.

Later she explained that the previous couple who had lived in that home had also separated and the husband had lived alone there for more than twenty years. The strength of the energy line below ground meant that even if a three-storey building was constructed on that site, it would affect the occupants on the top floor only slightly less than those on the ground floor. It was the type of power line that Indigenous Australians might have recognised and utilised during specific traditional ceremonies. A site like that with profound energy lines might be very effective for occasional rituals or ceremonies for heightening emotions but is not suitable for domestic life. The energy is too intense to for people who live close by.

The sheer power of this force is rare and not something most people consider when scanning a property before a purchase. For the right individual, perhaps someone focused on spiritual development, using the room at the front of that property as a meditation space might speed up personal growth. However, when meditating while feeling stressed or angry, a person is unlikely to enjoy deep, restful reflections. Environments can influence people in unseen ways.

After completing my readings for the day, I scanned my own property for energy lines and was relieved to find only two tunnels of light on the property. Energy tunnels offer easy access to spiritual energy for people who have difficulty finding it in meditation. They can be 10 to 30 or 40 centimetres across and are sometimes clearly felt if a person pauses briefly in the flow of a tunnel. They can be glimpsed in meditation if an individual scans for them.

Of course, these tunnels weren't conveniently placed for easy access. One was right on the corner of my office, more outside the building than inside whereas the other was beside an olive tree in the 17-acre park behind my home. The only way anyone might accidentally stumble across it would be by pushing through dense growth in search of a lost ball.

When intuitively scanning the entire park, I discovered a thin energy line similar to Kirsten's home near the entrance to the park in the next street. It wasn't as intense but it strengthens emotions slightly in the same way. As it isn't on a walking path, it's unlikely that anyone would spend extended periods immersed in its energy.

RETRIEVING INFORMATION USING MEDITATION

Receiving guidance or information during meditation is initially a hit-or-miss process but with practice, skills improve. Gradually, through repetition, individuals discover the most suitable forms of contemplation. Some people enjoy a solid 50 to 60 minutes in meditation to settle the mind, while for others, 15 minutes feels like an endurance test.

If you benefit from longer meditations, allow time at the end for taking notes. If you're more restless, ask questions early and end the session before your overactive mind has designed a boat, visualised how the kids are destroying the house without you or mentally made a dinner guest list for a party of 40. The length of each meditation has to work for you. Even fidgety people eventually find the best time of day to meditate and, with practice, can even extend their sessions. What matters is the relevance and accuracy of information retrieved during the process.

TIPS TO IMPROVE INTUITIVE MEDITATIONS

Before meditating, walk for 10 to 15 minutes, complete some yoga, gardening, stretching or light exercise to release tension.

Light a candle safely in the room before meditating. The fire improves the energy of the room slightly as it has a cleansing effect on the immediate surroundings. Extinguish the flame afterwards for safety reasons.

Weather permitting, open windows and doors before meditating to allow a breeze to remove any stagnant energy from the room.

If there are likely to be any noisy distractions (dogs barking, excited children squealing in a nearby swimming pool or traffic noise), play some soft, soothing music or white noise while meditating.

If your mind often wanders during meditation and fixates on unresolved issues, write a list of these issues before beginning. Then you can relax and forget them until your contemplation is complete.

If there is no possibility of escaping a crowded, noisy household, insert some earplugs or drive to a quiet park and meditate in the passenger seat of the car. It feels more spacious than the driver's seat and repetitive practice in the driver's seat can set up an association with meditation; not something you want when driving. Auditory people need quiet surroundings to focus when reflecting. Sometimes listening to repetitive sounds such as a ticking clock or waves crashing on a shore through earphones can remedy external distractions.

Forming simple habits before periods of mental stillness helps the physical body and mind prepare for the experience. Just as a bedtime ritual announces that it's time for sleep, playing soothing music or stretching before meditating encourages a relaxed, centred experience.

Sometimes for people who resist surrendering to light and stillness, the best meditations occur when they are physically exhausted. After collapsing into bed at the end of a long, arduous day, they have their most accurate psychic experiences, even in short periods of reflection. Because they are almost asleep at the beginning of the process, extending the progression usually leads to deep sleep. However, during those first few minutes, the physical body releases tension.

In this brief period of physical surrender, there is usually minimal resistance to spiritual energy. Consequently, a person is momentarily filled with light and able to accurately look ahead into the future. While most people have patchy meditations when they are tired, some discover that these are their best opportunities for intuitive glimpses of upcoming events. It's because they fleetingly release defences and surrender to spiritual light. This nurturing brightness settles the mind from racing or reacting to outside diversions. Mental distractions and an undisciplined mind are the most common complaints from people who struggle with deep, intuitive meditations.

Contemplating soon after vigorous exercise usually improves results, as can simple acceptance techniques. These include acknowledging each sound or distraction and then deliberately releasing it from conscious awareness. Mentally state something like the following when attempting to still the mind at home while other family members are in the home.

"I am aware of the loud television in the next room. I am aware of a dog barking. I accept it and release this sound. I am aware of traffic in the street downstairs and I let it go." This can be extended to include awareness of thoughts and of physical body sensations. It might include the following.

"I am aware of my heart beating. I am aware of thinking about work just now. I am aware of being distracted by my thoughts and I release them. I am aware of a breeze coming in through the open window and I let it go." Eventually, the mind settles and the stillness deepens. Breathing becomes rhythmic as the body settles into the process and the focus is centred on meditation.

When we are mentally and emotionally still, extended, deep meditations are nourishing for the mind, body and soul. Sometimes unexpectedly, a person experiences a 45-minute reflection that seemed like it lasted only a few minutes. In the profound peace, time seems to stand still. It's possible to feel so tranquil that all desire to ask questions evaporates. This is a state of grace. In these moments, we have all that we need and more. It is the peace that the spiritual aspects of people feel when released from the physical body each night during sleep. To experience this level of calm while awake is rare at first but with practice, it's possible to enjoy it daily. In this deep spiritual stillness, you can sense what your higher self knows about you, the world and the universe.

After these refreshing meditations, focus improves. It's as though a reset button is activated and ongoing stress is released. You feel a deep sense of lucidity and peace within. Decisions made soon afterwards are usually beneficial. This clarity can last a day or two. Be aware that your spiritual energy will be brighter for a period, attracting people who might unconsciously cord you or drain your energy. To remedy this, cleanse carefully for several days after a deep spiritual experience to prolong the positive feelings. You might swim in the ocean, take a salt bath, spend some time in nature or tackle a few gardening tasks. You're likely to be more creative and inspired for days after a deep, lucid meditation, so write down those original ideas while they are clear and fresh.

6. ASKING RISKY QUESTIONS

CLIENTS SOMETIMES ASK CLAIRVOYANTS, "WHEN WILL I DIE?" ON the surface, this is an innocent question that might help a person prepare for the inevitable. However, in reality, most individuals who learn this information have an internal clock ticking away, reminding them of another second or another minute they'll never have again as they move steadily towards the end of their time on earth. This unrelenting hourglass has more resonance if the person who expected to live into his nineties is told that he'll be gone at 61. It's a tricky question and most people are not prepared to hear the answer.

Only eternal optimists are likely to make the most of every hour of each day when they know how long life will be. More likely, this knowledge becomes a burden or a recipe for anxiety, with regrets about a life that hasn't fulfilled expectations. It can also become an excuse to squander more of those limited days remaining.

Instead of answering questions about the length of life, a better enquiry might include, "What will provide the most fulfilment in my remaining years?" Although people expect to be told about a personal quest, a spiritual pilgrimage or a chance to save the life of someone close, more often they are told to learn to play an instrument they dreamed of playing as a child, take up yoga or meditation or simply grow a garden. Although a personal quest might provide a milestone in life, positive daily habits and activities can yield ongoing nourishment throughout the years.

My neighbour, Nancy, is in her eighties. She is in her garden in all weather, in every season, from early morning — planting, pruning, weeding and mowing. Her daily efforts are rewarded with glorious blooms, fabulous fragrances, herbs and the pride of a job well done. I've seen people striding up the street away from the train station after work who pause at her fence for a moment to push their faces into a spray of roses or to breathe in the heady fragrance of a lawn covered in flowering freesias in spring. The rush to return home after a busy day is momentarily cast aside while they indulge their senses. Nancy's gardening efforts bring us all joy.

Asking about lasting happiness isn't usually centred on particular incidents. Its focus is what will bring you the deepest sense of fulfilment in your remaining years. As children, we are usually adept at discovering what makes us happy, yet sometimes as adults, we put aside these sources of joy to focus on daily responsibilities. Hobbies and personal pursuits don't need to be about perfecting skills. They can simply be fun to pursue.

In one reading, Sarah asked, "What major incidents in my life will provide spiritual or emotional insight?" This question suggests glimpses of adventures ahead of powerful meditations resulting in deep spiritual connections or personal mountains successfully conquered. The information received can arouse sufficient motivation for her to take up a new hobby or have lessons to learn a musical instrument. Alternatively, she might purchase a ticket to Saint-Jean-Pied-de-Port in France to commence the pilgrims' walk to Camino de Santiago in Spain. There are many different ways to lead fulfilling lives and sometimes psychic readings or deep meditations identify suitable paths to happiness. Often, it's something as simple as playing with grandchildren, helping others or supporting someone with a goal that brings the most joy.

ASKING SIGNIFICANT QUESTIONS

Using meditation to contact guides or to ask your higher self about important issues can be satisfying or sometimes disturbing, depending on individual comfort levels. Occasionally, it's necessary to establish personal boundaries around questions asked to prevent disappointment.

For example, if you're recently married and likely to become anxious about an unexpected answer, it's not prudent to ask about the long-term outcome of your relationship. This is why people consult experienced clairvoyants, who can help reconstruct their questions towards more rewarding outcomes.

It's a brave person who is prepared to ask absolutely any question and then live happily with the knowledge of likely outcomes. To avoid sleepless nights, depression or despair, it is advisable to set limits on specific information about future events. Most people instinctively understand what knowledge is sufficient and what can trigger anxiety or stress. Be careful with your enquiries.

Sometimes, when asking an enormous question that could have serious repercussions in your life, it might be more prudent to first pose this question: "Is it wise for me to ask my preferred question now?" If the answer is 'No', you might not be ready to hear what lies ahead. In a recent reading, a woman asked about her son's new business. Looking ahead, I saw Ben in his fifties, working for a corporation and enjoying the work. I then had to intuitively move back in time to find when he was likely to leave the business and why.

Ben had begun with passion and enthusiasm but gradually discovered success in his business required serious financial investment. If he borrowed hundreds of thousands of dollars, he'd be competing with companies with deeper pockets and more industry experience. He worked around 60 hours each week for less than his previous income. Consequently, his social life and health suffered. After a gruelling couple of years where he sacrificed weekends and missed social activities with friends, it was apparent that he could enjoy a better income with less effort by working for a company. Any initial regrets were soon extinguished by a stable income with supportive workmates. He was also free to go sailing with friends on Sundays. Blue skies and the salt air dissolved his weekday stress.

What people think they want to know is not always what they are ready to hear. Sometimes answering an emotionally loaded question triggers a pattern of worry and feelings of powerlessness over possible outcomes. When Carrie asked about becoming the head of department in her workplace, it was a role she had worked towards for over ten years. In her mind, this was her personal Mt Everest and she felt it was within her grasp. She spoke with excitement about her plans for the department and the possibilities ahead for team members, including job-sharing, ongoing training and permanent workplace coaches.

Looking ahead, I intuitively saw that the role would eventually be awarded to a man with less experience who was based in another department. He'd rely on Carrie to run the department while he spent his days in meetings. She was devastated at the news. Glancing at her phone, she realised that her entire list of questions revolved around her achieving this primary goal. To ensure that the session didn't drift, I intuitively scanned for more details.

Looking ahead further, I saw that she was likely to apply for positions in other organisations and accept one a few months after she missed out on that job. In her new position, she'd receive a promotion within two years and lead a team of five people who thrived together. In retirement, this new position was considered her most rewarding role in a long career. What initially looked like a setback was actually a nudge for her to get out of her comfort zone and find a better outcome. Opportunities sometimes arrive as frustrations or obstacles that test our skills and resourcefulness. It's through the process of stretching our capabilities that we prepare for new possibilities. Sometimes when people are acutely disappointed, they feel that they are broken. However, closer inspection and hindsight often reveal that those are growing pains, stretching them out of their comfort zones for new life chapters.

Occasionally, it's better to avoid giving clairvoyant readings to close friends or family members. A sibling might ask questions that could compromise your relationships with other people. If it is necessary to tell an acquaintance about a partner's infidelity, there is a risk of weakening that friendship. Sometimes, it's better to refer the person to another, more impartial reader for help.

CENSORING ANSWERS IN READINGS

Censoring what you say, even when not giving readings, is essential because if you're intuitive, people assume that many of your opinions are actually psychically based. This occurred when some friends came to stay for a week. Theo and Marcia arrived with their four-year-old daughter Skye and baby Tyler. Skye was a shy girl who followed her mother around for the whole visit, whereas Tyler wanted to independently explore his environment. Unable to walk and not yet crawling, he determinedly dragged himself across the floor, making his way around the house during the first afternoon. I needed to watch every step I took because he was never in the same place twice. It was like he was in training at a fitness camp.

Each time I walked past him, Tyler inclined his huge head to notice what I was doing. I figured that he was attempting an infant's version of mapping out his new environment by pacing it out. Unable to walk, he relied on his strong, tiny arms and frictionless clothing to navigate the polished wooden floors.

Tyler was so focused and persistent with his exploration goal, that I nicknamed him 'Mr Wilful'. The name stuck. "Where's Mr Wilful?" Marcia asked when we sat down to dinner. Weeks after they returned home, I received a text to announce that Mr Wilful had since learned to crawl and was currently attempting to break out of the house to explore the neighbourhood. I suggested that they attach a tracking device to alert them as to his current location. He is still referred to as Mr Wilful years later, despite now being a curious, conservative teenager. As a clairvoyant, sometimes a cheeky comment can be interpreted as an intuitive moment, so when developing intuition, strong filters are required before voicing personal observations.

7. SEEING THE BIG PICTURE OR TINY DETAILS

TO BETTER UNDERSTAND YOUR INTUITIVE SKILLSET, IT'S essential to determine if you have a macro or a micro viewpoint. Are you a big-picture person or a detail-oriented individual? If you're better suited to determining world events, it suggests a macro or big-picture perspective. If gleaning information about an individual's life is easier, you probably have a micro or detailed perspective. They are both useful but approach life from completely different viewpoints.

For individuals with a broader outlook, it's less complicated to focus on world events such as the global economy, political direction of countries and international trends. These intuitive people can see approaching recessions, climate changes and sometimes investment trends.

With a narrower focus, better results occur with personal predictions for individuals. This in-depth perspective can still provide information about worldwide events, but these are usually gleaned through personal predictions. If a person is employed in an industry that is undergoing change, it's possible to notice the wider transformation through the lens of a single person's life.

If someone plans to invest in shares of international organisations such as solar energy companies, it might help if the reader knows about world events to notice trends. This is better suited to a big-picture reader. However, if an individual wants information about a particular stock—whether it will increase by 5 or 10 per cent within 12 months—a detail-focused reader might be more effective.

THE MICRO VIEWPOINT

Sometimes a micro view provides glimpses of an individual's life ahead but lacks details about the path taken to arrive at the destination. Chloe was struggling to support four children after her husband left to marry a younger co-worker. Juggling her mortgage payments while working less than 20 hours per week meant that she was living hand-to-mouth. A good friend gave her a gift voucher for a birthday reading.

Scanning ahead ten years, I saw her with a gathering of friends in the kitchen of a home where she lived. I described the large kitchen with pale stone benchtops. She shook her head and told me that it wasn't the kitchen in her current house. I looked more closely and as she seemed to be the host, I guessed it was her next house.

Many of the people around her were work colleagues, and there was a warm, convivial atmosphere. The gleaming appliances and beautiful surroundings suggested Chloe was financially stable and her neat surroundings and confident, relaxed manner in the image presented a direct contrast to the dishevelled, weary woman currently slumped in front of me.

I clairvoyantly saw her working full-time in a different industry where she felt appreciated by her company. It seemed her current impoverished circumstances were simply a difficult chapter in her life. Ten years ahead, Chloe seemed to be more confident and content with her life and happily single.

"Amen to that," she said when I told her this. "Who needs a husband when you have a dog?" she laughed. "But how do I get to there from here?"

"The first step is to give up pursuing a career in the industry you currently work in. You aren't valued there. It's time to use your skills and talents where they are more appreciated."

"Very helpful. You've just taken me from 15 to 20 hours of work per week to zero."

"On the contrary," I reminded her. "I've just set you a task to complete over the coming months. You might need to learn some different skills for the new direction once you've found it. If you can manage four children, you can steer yourself towards a bright new career. Perhaps that's why your friend gave you this gift voucher, to help you discover the potential in yourself that she already sees in you."

This is the micro view. If I had been taking a broader view, I might have told Chloe that her industry was being less valued and burdened under governance and compliance in the coming decade and that it was now time to get out. She obviously had too much passion and enthusiasm for an industry that valued only conformity.

A micro perspective includes examining the client's character traits, strengths and weaknesses. In a recent reading, a woman enquired about love relationships ahead. Nicola had not been in a long-term relationship for over ten years. Her current on/off relationship with Joe wasn't progressing and she was exhausted from focusing on possibilities that weren't likely to eventuate. Given her age, I sensed there wasn't time to sugar-coat the answer, so I took a deep breath and laid it out for her.

"There are two paths ahead for you," I said. "Neither of these include Joe. Joe is a nice guy, but he's not featuring in your future. If you put additional effort into this partnership, it will simply erode more precious years of your life." She nodded dejectedly.

"And the two paths?"

"If you continue on path one, there are two more love relationship opportunities ahead, but both leave you feeling empty, just as you feel right now. They are not bad people, just the same type of men you've pursued in the past who are offering similar results." I sensed she wanted the second path to be easy, perfect and long-lasting. I felt bound to inform her that her happiness depended on personal effort to transform herself. In doing this, she might discover that a relationship was only one avenue to fulfilment for her and not her sole source of happiness.

"The second path requires effort and commitment from you to resolve some past issues and emotional patterns. Without this personal determination, you're likely to meet a third man but let him go and miss a great opportunity for love." I paused again, aware that this was a lot of information to assimilate and that she needed to absorb it bit by bit.

"The second path involves finding a counsellor to work with on personal issues from childhood. You have an old template of what constitutes a love relationship that needs to be updated. You'll actually consult three different counsellors, searching for the right fit for you. The first one is a woman who is too clinical for you. Her pursed lips and slightly raised eyebrow leave you feeling like a naughty schoolgirl. The second is too self-centred for you. You like him but basically, he's simply another man who can't look beyond himself to notice you."

Nicola looked slightly alarmed at the long road ahead but I sensed that deep down, she knew that her life template was not working but didn't know how to change it. I continued before she became overwhelmed by the effort needed.

"The third counsellor is a gentle-natured man with a shaved head. He's softly spoken, kind and tolerant but gradually, you come to understand that he doesn't miss anything you say and also understands much of what you leave out, both deliberately and unconsciously. Slowly, he begins to call you on your justifications for personal actions. He asks you if you want to change the world or yourself."

"If you persevere with him, you'll be well prepared for the third opportunity when it arrives. Basically, you'll be ready to be heard and loved. This relationship will be unlike anything you've had in your life. From an outsider's perspective, it isn't fireworks or gondola rides in Venice — but when others observe you together, they see two happy people with mutual respect and patient kindness for each other."

"Can I ask a different question about Joe?" She hadn't fully comprehended the information, but she'd probably understand more deeply when listening to her recording later.

The risk of finding Mr or Ms Perfect when feeling personally inadequate is that the new partner might make you feel awkward or fearful of losing what you have found. Perhaps Joe was already Nicola's perfect man, yet unavailable, disinterested and absorbed in his own life. He was possibly a replica of Nicola's father, focused on his own needs while oblivious to hers. Joe was a familiar type to her and the counselling process seemed necessary to help Nicola move beyond what was a comfortable habit towards a more nurturing relationship. Valuing what you bring to friendships and relationships helps when negotiating to have your needs met. If someone doesn't appreciate your personal contribution, self-confidence is required to move on in search of a more suitable partner.

LIMITATIONS TO THE MICRO VIEWPOINT

A micro viewpoint has its limits. Before the Australian federal election in 2011, I took some time to look ahead to see who was likely to win the election. My process (flawed, as it turned out) was to search ahead to the evening of the election to see each contender addressing the press and supporters. In previous elections, it was a straightforward process to determine the winner as one candidate usually presented with a sense of victory when addressing his or her team, while the other seemed exhausted. It's easy to recognise someone putting on a brave face.

On the evening of this election, neither candidate seemed jubilant. Reasoning that there might be delays with vote counting, I clairvoyantly moved forward 24 hours and still there was no apparent winner and loser. I ventured forward two more days, believing that it wasn't possible to go this long without a winner being declared but there was still no obvious outcome. I was puzzled until the actual election came and went without a clear winner. After much negotiation between the main parties and independent politicians, a winner was finally declared more than ten days later. To redress this flaw in my election prediction process, in future I'll look ahead one month and then two months. I'll search newspaper headlines and see which candidate's face is more prominent in the news.

It's important to know when to search for narrow or broad information about a situation. Specific details involve noticing that your client will have a respiratory illness in six months while a wide viewpoint occurs when you're aware that almost everyone in her neighbourhood has the same illness and that it's likely that a virus is sweeping through the community.

THE MICRO VIEWPOINT USED IN HEALTH READINGS

Health readings often require a micro viewpoint if the reader wants to examine the physical body in sections or through body systems like the circulatory system, nervous system, etc. In a reading for Selma, I noticed a tremor in her left hand. She seemed too young to have had a stroke, so I intuitively looked for any incident or health issue that might explain it. Tracing its origins, it appeared to have manifested after a car accident 12 years earlier. I hadn't noticed it when she sat down but it was apparent during a scan of her body.

"Do you sometimes notice a tremor in your left hand?" I asked.

"Yes, it comes and goes."

"How long have you had it?"

"Ten years, or more."

"Did you experience a shock or an injury to that left shoulder around twelve years ago? You would have been around age 30."

"Yes. We were driving in a freak snowstorm and my partner lost control of the vehicle. We spun out sideways and hit a parked car. It was a shock but we were okay."

"Yes, it could have been worse but that accident appears to be related to your tremor. Could you see a physiotherapist about that? If not, a chiropractor might help."

Each viewpoint (macro and micro) has its strengths and weaknesses and it's possible to switch from one to the other. However, most people prefer one method.

Sometimes both the micro and macro approaches are required in a single reading. The method with a narrow focus allows for specific details, such as current health issues, whereas the broad viewpoint can help if you need to scan back year by year, to find causes for current conditions. The macro system is good for broad scanning, so that the client isn't bored while the clairvoyant slowly scans back forty years to find a source.

THE MACRO PERSPECTIVE

A macro perception of life is suitable for television interviews where an individual can predict the outcome of an election, by focusing on an electoral party rather than an individual. It's also good for gauging the economic direction of a country or weather patterns for the coming year in a particular region. The micro view is more applicable for personal predictions but even these can be tricky. There's a fine line between seeing a likely future for a client and imagining a possible outcome.

In a recent meditation on Australia's political future, I was surprised to foresee the emergence of a new political party, gradually capturing 34% of the primary vote. As this party gained traction, the established two-party system would lose its dominance, diminishing the power of the old parties. Examining a political landscape (not individual politicians) this way is a macro viewpoint. As this is not my natural strength, it requires more concentration and centredness to be accurate. I naturally favour the micro approach.

MACRO VIEWPOINT — STRENGTHS

- Glimpsing national and international trends.
- Locating best markets for new products.
- Tracing weather patterns, noticing how rainfall affects crops and farming investments.
- Looking ahead at general trends in finance, politics, fashion or travel.
- Determining the best worldwide location for a person or business to thrive.
- Noticing how political changes or financial investments affect countries' and citizens' quality of life.

MACRO VIEWPOINT — WEAKNESSES

- Being unable to pinpoint an individual's opportunities within an overall trend.
- A person might not benefit from a particular investment despite others profiting from a particular trend.
- Less focus on the client suggests that this is unsuitable for most personal readings.
- Unlikely to pinpoint an individual's opportunities within a fashion or a trend.

MICRO VIEWPOINT — STRENGTHS

- Better suited to personal readings and predictions.
- Takes into account the client's talents, strengths and weaknesses when looking ahead at opportunities. Sometimes a job we might thrive in doesn't use current skills but requires existing strengths or talents.
- It's possible to zoom in on particular incidents, issues or turning points in a person's life to see how a different decision might lead to a more rewarding outcome.
- A micro reader can recognise what an individual is receiving from a relationship or a situation and identify what else might provide the same nourishment without debilitating compromises.
- When searching for answers, most people are less concerned with humanity and more preoccupied with their own fulfilment. This approach provides a deep, personal focus.

MICRO VIEWPOINT — WEAKNESSES

- Not suitable for exploring world markets for ideas or products without examining each individual market.

- The reader sometimes glimpses situations without context. This can leave clients feeling nervous if they don't realise that what has been seen is 'the new normal' in life ahead. For example, a reader glimpses the client leaving their last job when they are 50 years of age and not working again. However, a broader examination might reveal that they inherited a block of apartments and could live comfortably on their property investment income.
- Glimpsing specific incidents can miss the overall theme of an individual's life. A reader might describe seeing the client in an old cottage in the heart of the country and the client assumes that this is where they will live. However, it might be a home they rent for an annual holiday to give them a break from their modern city apartment.
- Taking a close-up view of a person's life doesn't always reveal how an individual develops personal beliefs or why particular life dreams are abandoned or permanently compromised.
- Sometimes when zooming in on a particular issue or behaviour it's easy to miss surrounding influences and the consequences of changing this behaviour. This occurs when a clairvoyant glimpses a scene of the client overseas and presumes they are on holiday, whereas they might have travelled for a christening, a conference or a funeral.

In a clairvoyant reading with a micro viewpoint, a client might ask, "What does the future hold for my business in the next two years?" However, an occupational question addressed to a reader with a macro perspective might be phrased as, "What does the future hold for my industry over the next two years?" Knowing the direction of your particular industry can help you keep ahead of the competition or decide when to change career direction. In recent decades, we have seen the demise of record stores, video shops, a large percentage of bookstores and many family manufacturing businesses. Instead, we download music, watch films through apps on our devices and more people have swapped reading paperbacks for audiobooks. For some, it's a luxury to have someone read to us as we go about our daily chores. For others, life is too demanding to have it any other way.

A predicted slump in the economy is likely to result in a downturn in the client's business. Knowing that there is a countrywide contraction can alert the person to avoid embarking on expensive expansion plans and instead, pay down debt. With a more finely focused question, such as, "What product or service will help my business through this approaching fiscal winter?" the reader can pinpoint a specific product, opportunity or service that is likely to be in demand despite a downturn.

In a recent pure clairvoyance reading, Dana asked about her 10-year-old son Mischa. She explained Mischa had been diagnosed with Autism Spectrum Disorder and that he loved to paint. I began by describing his companion dog, a pre-trained poodle cross who was gradually becoming his best friend. Every couple of minutes, the dog looked up to see what he was doing and would be by his side immediately if Mischa left the room. They were becoming inseparable and Mischa loved his constant companion.

"Where does the dog currently sleep?" I asked Dana.

"In the laundry," she replied.

"Not for long," I replied. I clairvoyantly saw the dog, determined to be part of the family, sharing Mischa's bed and loving all the soft space available to him. Both child and animal were delighted with their new arrangement.

Dana asked about her son's career as an adult. Images of Mischa painting and drawing leaves momentarily distracted me. Leaves of every size, shape and shade of green, russet and orange filled large pages. They ranged from deep cherry red, to dusty olive and luminescent yellow greens with every vein visible. The details were exquisite. Larger than life, they were hyper-realistic.

Shifting forward to glimpse Mischa in his late twenties, he was a psychologist in private practice. His natural affinity for noticing patterns had been carefully channelled into observing human habits and behaviours. He specialised in art therapy with children and teenagers. In a particular session with a young boy aged around eight, they stood together in silence on a cotton drop sheet in his office, each painting a canvas. Earlier attempts were strewn across the fabric beneath their feet while they stood, intently focused on their individual efforts.

After 30 minutes, Mischa asked the child to explain to him the significance of his painting. The boy stood in silence for a few moments, carefully wiping residual paint from the tip of his brush with a piece of cloth. He spoke softly at first, as though anticipating disinterest or even a scolding from Mischa. Instead, Mischa listened attentively, nodding to assure the child that he understood each description. Eventually, the boy became more confident, describing his dog, pet rabbits, a hole in the wooden fence where his dog sometimes squeezed out to sneak off to the park, the noisy washing machine and the soothing sounds of the tumble dryer that helped him fall asleep at night. He tentatively described the scary neighbour on one side and a friendly old lady on the other, who sometimes gave him eggs from her chickens.

When it was Mischa's turn to explain his own painting, he spoke in a soft, soothing voice, methodically wiping flecks of paint from his spectacles with a fine cloth while describing the boy's current emotional and mental life patterns. He knew that his young client might go home and dream about their session that night. The subconscious mind is a powerful tool for absorbing new concepts that increase inner strength and resilience. Mischa deliberately mentioned a new possible way to move the child's life forward, capitalising on his particular individual strengths. He was consciously planting positive seeds in the boy's mind that might grow into constructive ideas and foundational beliefs in later life. The gentle man was a welcome ray of sunshine in an otherwise bleak period of this child's life. Mischa was careful not to intrude into the boy's world as he provided a welcome connection to a lonely child who was ignored by his classmates and by the neighbourhood children.

Mischa's clients thought he was simply an artist, but he instinctively glimpsed layers of emotional and mental patterns and represented them in story form while they painted. In those silent periods, as the sunlight gradually moved around the room, he'd carefully sift through what he heard and what he sensed with each fellow painter.

He was basically showing these young individuals their own unique qualities that others did not yet appreciate or value. Because they weren't sitting opposite him in a chair being asked questions, his clients felt relaxed enough to reveal themselves to Mischa. His office provided a sanctuary in weeks filled with deadlines, demands, judgements and noisy chaos.

After I mentioned this to his mother, Dana smiled gratefully. “It looks like he’ll be fine,” she murmured, leaning back into her chair, sighing with relief.

8. IS THIS GOOD NEWS OR BAD NEWS?

NO ONE WANTS BAD NEWS. A SMALL NUMBER OF PEOPLE FEAR developing personal intuition in case they glimpse a bad outcome and cannot stop it. The answer to this is to look closely at the results of efforts during intuitive processes, noticing if you seem happy with them. It's dispiriting to intuitively look ahead at a new personal venture and see it abandoned in a year or two. Sometimes a new project pursued has a deeper, underlying spiritual purpose that, once discovered, makes the original goal unnecessary. This occurred to me in 1988 on a trip to Europe. I planned to land in London and then explore a range of countries including Switzerland, France, Italy, Greece and Ireland. Instead, I worked for five of the six months I was away from home in a small psychic centre in London. I was there to meet a spiritual teacher, who opened my eyes to what was possible if a person pursued spiritual development and not simply intuitive practices.

On the flight home, I was disappointed not to have explored Switzerland but grateful to have met Christine. Had I intuitively seen the outcome before the trip, I might not have taken the journey as it didn't fulfil my plans. It was a reminder that life doesn't always announce the plans it has for us.

Another reason for not wanting to improve intuitive abilities is to avoid delivering bad news to friends, family members or to strangers. In professional practice, intuitive readers eventually become proficient at delivering unwelcome information.

Palmistry, a whole-life reading, sometimes reveals particular points in a person's life where there will be fewer new jobs, relationships, travels or adventures. Rather than becoming fixated on the end-of-life process, it's important to remember that what we take with us from this journey are the memories of what we did while alive. Being aware of this can help us immerse ourselves in the immediate opportunities and positive experiences that daily existence provides.

It is impossible to know with certainty that specific information is likely to be upsetting. What might be overwhelming news to one person could be a timely wake-up call for another. Some twists or turns in life are the short-term results of sudden decisions. Others, however, have warning signs along the path.

A recent client, Frank, asked about investment in a small country hotel that his brother, Kerry, suggested buying. Kerry was a builder and had worked in hospitality previously, so it sounded promising. I had to tell him this was not a stable investment. To help Frank make his own decision, I clarified by explaining that Kerry was likely to occasionally present other investment opportunities, but it was important that he carefully consider each one on its merits, politely declining any that didn't seem right for him.

"There is no sense in wasting money simply to make your brother happy," I said.

"I've already done that with a previous shared investment that collapsed, costing us tens of thousands of dollars each," he replied.

Sometimes when readers say 'No' to a person's dreams and plans, they might initially disappoint their clients. It's important to remember that the reader might also be saving these same people from mounting debt, lost friendships or even ongoing law suits.

Occasionally, clients exercise personal free will and ignore the reader's predictions, sometimes returning months afterwards with another list of possible investments. Past experience has shown that when people disregard accurate advice they have paid for, they often need additional readings to answer questions about how they can limit their losses or exposure to risk. At that point, it's sometimes too late to undo the damage. This is why professionals record their sessions — to give clients the option to revisit readings later and hear what wasn't fully absorbed the first time.

On rare occasions, astute people pursue their goals while being vigilant about the pitfalls predicted, determined to find solutions for each obstacle. It is possible to successfully change predicted outcomes by not taking the exact steps glimpsed by the clairvoyant. This usually involves carefully observing personal choices, turning points and people who can provide support towards desired goals. Caution about the possible consequences of decisions or actions is important to avoid costly mistakes.

When telling someone that pursuing a particular love relationship is not a wise course of action, it's important to explain why. Recently, Veronica asked about the future of her 12-year relationship with Rudy. They had met when Veronica was in her late thirties but now, she was distraught.

The cards on the table repeatedly showed children but she didn't have any. I intuitively scanned back into her life to see if she wanted a family but was denied this for some reason. She had grown up expecting to have children but when she met Rudy, he told her that he wasn't ready for a family.

On closer inspection, he never wanted a family and it seemed to me that he knew that if he delayed his commitment to her until she reached her mid-forties it wouldn't seem like he had prevented her from having a child. Instead of stating this aloud, I asked Veronica a few questions.

"What age were you when you met Rudy?"

"Thirty-eight."

"Was Rudy hesitant about getting married at first?"

"Yes, a bit," she replied. I knew that the answer to the next question was to be forty-five or forty-six but I asked it anyway.

"What age were you when you moved in to live together?"

"Forty-six."

"And did you want to have a family?"

"Yes. It was too late by then."

I glanced ahead to see another man arriving in her life in two years. When I told her this, she seemed shocked and afraid of this possibility.

"What will happen to Rudy and me?"

"The choice is yours when the new man arrives," I replied. "If you are still content with Rudy, you can thank the new man for his attention and tell him you're not interested. It's good to have more opportunities than you need."

"As I see it, you have three choices. First, you can say 'No' and send him on his way. Life with Rudy then sails along as before. Second, you can have an affair with the new man without leaving Rudy, but this is likely to become stressful and complicated. Third, you can leave Rudy and pursue a new relationship."

"Why on earth would I choose to do that?"

"You might do that if the new man offers you something that Rudy doesn't."

"Like what?" she asked earnestly.

"The new man offers you his full attention. He is prepared to negotiate to meet your needs and his desire is to keep everyone happy. He'll also see your potential and help you live some of it. Does Rudy do this for you?" She didn't answer this question, but her expression showed she knew the answer. I continued. "There is another possibility, of course."

"What's that?"

"The unexpected man might be a wake-up call for Rudy. When you are approached by someone new who wants you to thrive, Rudy can choose to step up and do the same or let you go, knowing that you're moving on to a better life."

Sitting opposite Veronica and looking back 12 years and then forward another three, it was apparent that she was stuck, silently hoping that Rudy might become the man of her dreams. Meanwhile, Rudy was already living his perfect, child-free life, making every holiday a camping trip or leaving her behind while he went fishing for the weekend.

It was likely that when the new man arrived, she'd breathe freely and step forward without a backward glance. She wasn't yet ready to hear that. As this was a clairvoyant reading, it wasn't my place to make her ready. Instead, I reminded myself that I am simply a witness, briefly invited to peer into the lives of others and describe what I can see.

While sitting with me, Veronica interpreted it as bad news. I was attempting to tell her that all those years of silently hoping and holding her breath were futile. The prospect of a fresh relationship upset her because she viewed it as threatening the safety of her current situation; but I had also told her that someone was coming who would truly see her, appreciate what she had to offer, and genuinely want her to thrive. I had described the spring to follow her current winter. When the opportunity arrives, the choices will still be Veronica's. It will probably be painful to let go of a long-term dream — but perhaps the new option might be easier than she expects.

When I have to tell a client that they won't purchase the house they love, or are unlikely to be offered a dream job or meet their perfect partner anytime soon, I usually encourage them to ask more specific qualifying questions such as:

- Will I find a more suitable home to purchase in the next four months?
- Is it wise to expand my search area for the perfect home?
- Is it best to study or prepare more carefully for the right job for me?
- Is it necessary to take a short-term job while preparing for my next long-term position?
- What do I need to resolve from my past to be ready for my perfect love relationship?

Predictions are not simply about telling someone what is likely to happen in the coming months or years. They are an opportunity to explore a range of paths and possibilities before having to commit time, money or effort to particular goals. Being forewarned about an approaching personal winter allows a chance to prepare for lean times ahead. It's also important to offer a description of the spring that follows the approaching winter, to provide motivation during bleak periods.

Many years ago, a client asked me about her health and I had to deliver bad news. Although it was a blow to her, Fabiola wasn't completely surprised. She had already undergone several surgical procedures to remove cancerous tissue, including one eye and part of a lung. She paused for a moment, summoning courage and steeling herself before asking a specific health question.

"Did my recent surgery remove all of the cancer in my body?" I had noticed a slight tremor in her frail hand while she selected each card, as she sat, perched forward on the chair like a small child. Glancing down at the layout, it wasn't positive. From the cards she had selected, it appeared the answer was 'No'.

I explained what I saw and urged her to check with her doctor or medical specialist for absolute confirmation. She mentioned she was having regular, ongoing tests. I then intuitively scanned her body and noticed some spots in her lungs and in other areas. Over the next few years, Fabiola regularly returned for readings, courageously asking the same question. The answer was identical each time. I had to be honest with her despite my wish for her to be well, so that she could examine her options and make realistic plans. She died three years after her first reading, leaving behind her husband and her eight-year-old son. I was invited to her service. It was heart-wrenching to meet the people Fabiola had left behind, those I'd only intuitively seen in her readings.

It was a reminder that psychically glimpsing outcomes is not the same as experiencing them directly. Readers are usually removed from the grief and loss resulting from actual events. However, they still need to treat clients with patience, compassion and honesty and resist the temptation to collude with them that everything will eventually be fine. Sometimes outcomes are painful and people need to prepare for challenges ahead.

When predicting difficult times ahead, readers sometimes hope they are mistaken. However, maybe Fabiola's readings helped her to make solid preparations for the end of her life. After one reading, she told me she had written out 13 birthday cards for her son, one for each year until his 21st birthday. I felt overwhelmed by her calmness in the face of adversity and afterwards miserably reminded myself that clairvoyants are only witnesses — we cannot change the future.

9. INTUITIVELY SCANNING ANIMALS

WHEN I FIRST MET MY WIFE, SHE HAD A YOUNG CAT, ZOE. SHE HAD been rescued at 12 months of age and my wife had no history of Zoe's first year. When I arrived, Zoe ran away from me whenever she saw me. She bolted from all men, suggesting possible mistreatment by a man at some stage.

In the first year of our relationship, I sometimes spent an afternoon at my wife's house to let in tradesmen, servicemen or to accept important deliveries. On these days, I was instructed to feed Zoe. Upon arrival, I was usually met with a look that said, "Oh no! It's the man. Not only that but this means that soon there will be other, louder men with tools, hammers, electric saws and noisy phones."

One day, I noticed Zoe had decided that if I fed her, I would become tolerable, in that 'day-shift housekeeper' kind of way. I was useful. As the months progressed, Zoe sometimes sat happily on the other end of the sofa for an hour or two, until my partner arrived home. At this time, Zoe would suddenly flee, seemingly terrified by 'the man'. I fixed her double standard quickly by not feeding her immediately when I arrived. Instead, I reminded her I was a scary man and with this in mind, she really ought to be absconding from me. Eventually, when I arrived at the door the escaping ceased. She gave me a dismissive look — "Oh it's you; and about time too. I'm starving."

For over ten years, the three of us have lived in the same house, but Zoe still treats me like I'm a second-rate housekeeper in training, who's simply maintaining the home until Melinda returns home after work. When Melinda goes away for work for a few days, Zoe often sits at the bottom of the 30-metre driveway staring searchingly into the dark for a sign that her real owner might return soon. It's heartbreaking but no amount of reassurance from me placates her.

I decided one night that if she didn't understand my words, perhaps I might explain more easily to her in meditation. That night, after she had spent an hour out on the drive, I met with her in meditation to explain that her real owner was away and that she missed her and wanted to be home with her. I reminded her that Melinda would be home again soon (in five days or about 23 sleeps). The following morning, Zoe seemed more relaxed. That evening, she didn't sit out on the drive expectantly. Instead, she slept peacefully by the open fire as she did on any other crisp June night.

READING FOR AN UNFAMILIAR ANIMAL

Recently, I was training a student in animal communication using photos of pets emailed to me by friends and clients. Reading for unfamiliar animals is a suitable test of accuracy. The only information we have for these practice sessions is an image of the animal, plus the name, gender and the current age of the particular pet.

Kim was an enthusiastic student, sometimes impatient to get through as many different animals in a one-hour lesson as possible. However, I realised that this was training for future readings to be given to clients in an office or on the phone, each taking 30 to 60 minutes. In one lesson, I produced an image of a large ginger-and-white cat. This enormous animal was sprawled out across a table looking like the proverbial fat cat. Kim studied the picture for a few minutes, ignoring the two-page form I had prepared for him to fill out as he went. The form listed the organs, the digestive system, the heart and other body parts to ensure that students don't overlook anything.

"Does this cat suffer with conjunctivitis regularly?" he asked me.

"How would I know?" I wondered, remaining silent to avoid interrupting his concentration. My role was to provide structure to the session, not to act as a clairvoyant. He spoke quickly for three minutes about the hip joints, possible issues with mobility due to excess weight in years to come, the animal's state of mind and attitude to its environment. He then pushed the photo back across the table to me, happy with the results.

"That's good but what about the rest of the hour?"

"Sorry?"

"That was a solid three minutes but as a client, I'd expect you to talk about my pet for at least 45 minutes. If I leave now, I'm likely to feel that the session was too short or that you didn't say enough."

"But what about the accuracy?" he asked.

"I can't assess your precision yet because I don't know this animal. We'll phone the owner in a moment and you can list your findings aloud and gauge your success by her comments and reactions as you go. Perhaps before phoning her, you might like to consider all the un-ticked boxes on the animal-reading form."

I knew that his youthful impatience to assess the next animal was partly due to his smooth fingers (a palmistry observation, see left image below), which usually indicates a changeable, impulsive, intuitive nature. They also signify someone who prefers the bigger picture to the minute details of a particular situation. These fingers are relatively smooth from tip to base without swelling around the knuckles. They are essentially macro viewpoint readers.

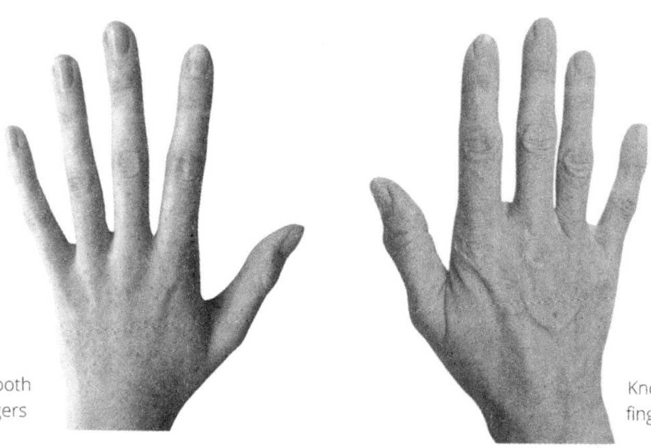

Smooth fingers

Knotty fingers

The image on the right shows a hand with knotty fingers. Knotty-fingered people usually enjoy immersing themselves into the details of a subject but can sometimes overlook the bigger picture. Notice how the fingers in the knotty hand swell slightly around the knuckles. If in doubt about your own hands, trace around one hand onto a piece of white paper and see for yourself.

I encouraged Kim to flesh out his animal reading for more precision, without repeating himself. To help with this I added a few lines to the printed form for future lessons. These included:

- When speaking to the client, ask if they have any specific questions about the animal.
- Enquire if the person understands what has been said to avoid confusion.
- Ask if there are any other animals at home. If so, take a moment to see how the pet you're currently scanning is affected by other animals in the immediate surroundings.
- If there are issues between this and other animals in the home environment, explore why this is happening and when it first occurred. Discovering the origins of an issue or behaviour can help the person understand the pet more clearly.

When Kim spoke to Monty's owner, Kylie, the conversation flowed more easily because Kylie was eager to talk about her cat, ask a few questions and know more about some of Monty's personality quirks. After the call ended, Kim seemed very pleased with himself and enthusiastic about the possibilities. He spoke rapidly, waving his hands around excitedly as he explained what he had said to the client, as though I wasn't there to observe.

"That was good. She confirmed many of your findings and you provided some solid information that she can check with the vet next time she visits." Kim was already clutching another image, eager to move on to a new animal and to speak with the owner while I was aware of the short duration of the reading.

"How long do you think the whole process took?" I asked him, while he stared intently at the image in his hand.

"Which process?"

"How long do you estimate you spent with the animal reading from the time I gave you the photo until the phone call with the owner ended?

"Forty minutes?"

"Actually, it was 13 minutes." I wasn't deliberately trying to quell his enthusiasm but to simply remind him to be more aware of the clock throughout the process. If he planned to offer 45-minute telephone sessions for animal scanning, it was better to learn to pace himself from the beginning.

Next, we considered an image of an 11-year-old dog named Tingo. Kim filled in his animal body scan form before I phoned Tingo's owner so that he could practise pacing himself in how he delivered his findings. Clara, Tingo's owner, was excited to hear about her dog's health, his behavioural issues and his relationship with different family members. Kim was spurred on by having immediate confirmation of some of the descriptions he gave during this 15-minute phone call and later wished he'd had more time to take more notes before the phone call.

We agreed that in future, after completing the form, we'd review it and then take another five minutes to focus on the animal while expanding his notes before phoning the owner. I reminded him to slow down, as the client was hearing what he had to say for the first time. We had extended the reading process, but it was still well short of the 45 minutes he'd need to achieve a complete reading. Although part of the reading was taking place before the phone call to the owner, there needed to be more phone conversation time, because that's what the client is likely to remember.

Eventually, the animal readings included some quiet time to scan the animal using a photograph before a 30–40-minute phone call to discuss findings with the animal's owner. During practice sessions, it was less stressful for Kim to spend more time scanning quietly with a shorter time on the phone. As he became more confident with the process, we gradually extended the phone part of the readings. Having a set period to focus only on one particular animal helped increase his accuracy. In his final sessions, he was introduced to clients who wanted two or three animals scanned in a single session.

Readers often experience increased stress levels just prior to a session. They worry about accuracy or clients who may not be able to relate to anything they are saying or that they might not have anything useful to say. Talkative readers usually overcome this stress as soon as the conversation with clients begins and they enter the flow of the reading. At that point, the process resembles a conversation between two people, especially when clients feel that they can interrupt the reader with questions to clarify important points.

Shy readers might experience extended periods of stress during sessions because they tend to say less. For introverted practitioners, it's important to remember that pet owners are sometimes silent because they are taking notes or making sense of what is being said. With experience, clairvoyants who are shy and empathetic are better able to begin the process where people are in their lives presently. When clients relax, psychics with strong empathy can gradually change the pace of the reading and direct it where it needs to go while sensing the comfort levels of patrons throughout the process.

During the next few lessons with Kim, additional boxes were added to the scanning charts. Kim steadily improved his reading process and timing, by checking that the form was fully completed before phoning to present his findings. He discovered that people were happy to talk about their animals and that the extended telephone time passed rapidly when he was fully focused on the owner and the pet. As expected, his early nerves dissipated as he became more confident in his abilities and comfortable with the process. Eventually, my role was that of a timekeeper as Kim's readings flowed more smoothly. We'd review each client session afterwards, further refining his reading process.

In one lesson, Tracy requested a follow-up session after a pet's behaviour changed in relation to other animals in the home. This reading focused on the dynamics of three dogs in one household, where the smallest dog was bullying the middle-sized one. The little old Jack Russell terrier, Ollie, didn't enjoy sharing his space with other dogs. The middle dog, Jackie, is an active Border collie and the largest is Ruby, a huge, fluffy, long-haired German shepherd. Ollie sleeps regularly throughout the day and often growls at Jackie, who is curious, manic and hyperactive. Ruby loves to visit the park and barks only when it's absolutely necessary. Kim determined that Jackie often disturbed the little dog during naps, so he suggested Tracy allow access to a private resting room for Ollie, out of reach of the others. A few months later, Tracy emailed to thank Kim for his suggestion. Ollie was much better behaved when he knew he had a private place to retreat to when he needed to rest.

When clients phoned about pets with serious health issues or when animal readings occurred during health crises, Kim remained calm, attentive and patient. It definitely helped that he was also a qualified veterinary surgeon and was familiar with a wide range of animals and health issues. He was careful not to diagnose during readings, instead tactfully suggesting that clients take their pets to a local qualified vet when he sensed that this was required.

The added benefit of giving readings on a speaker phone while being supervised was that Kim could iron out the repetition of words like "*um*" and "*er*" and other bad habits. As he became more experienced and word spread about the animal readings, I was being swamped by pet owners to be put on the list for animal scans during Kim's lessons. Eventually, Kim set a small fee for readings given under supervision to offset the cost of his lessons.

This intuitive training is likely to benefit Kim when an animal arrives at his veterinary clinic unconscious or with serious injuries and he needs to locate the issues as quickly as possible. In emergency situations, there is greater pressure to be accurate than in phone readings because of the gravity of the situation plus the pet owner's heightened state of anxiety.

Try it for yourself. Begin with your own pet, who might be sleeping in another room, or study a clear photograph of an animal. Don't work with a tiny photo or one containing several people and animals because this can lead to confusion. Humans throughout history have always talked to their animals but many don't realise that communication is a two-way street. Using intuition, it's possible to become aware of your animal's needs and preferences.

ANIMAL ASSESSMENT PROCESS

1. Set aside 15 to 20 minutes for this technique, preferably in a quiet place where you are unlikely to be distracted or disturbed.
2. Hold one or several clear photos of a particular animal in one hand and focus solely on the pet. This can be a printed photo or a digital image on a phone or tablet. Make sure it is clearly visible.
3. Work your way slowly down the Animal Body Scan Chart (see following page). You can find printable versions of this list online at www.paulfentonsmith.com/downloads to record your findings.
4. If you're working with a friend's pet, it's best to phone the owner to discuss the results. Don't simply email your conclusions because sometimes a conversation clarifies a particular situation. It is also helpful to have the owner confirm your findings, as this increases confidence for future animal readings.
5. Take notes as the conversation unfolds. These might include additional information you've given the owner and questions asked by the pet's carer. You can tick each area that the owner confirms as accurate. Explain that you cannot diagnose illnesses or conditions and any health areas mentioned need to be physically checked by a veterinarian.
6. File each page in a folder for easy reference and ensure you have a few blank forms printed and ready to go for your next animal assessment.

ANIMAL BODY SCAN CHART

Slowly and carefully scan down through the body areas listed below, noting anything unusual. Take more time with any inconsistencies or areas that register tension, lack of blood flow or sensitivity.

Animal's Name: ____________________ Age: _____ Gender: _____

- Skull
- Brain
- Eyes
- Strength of vision in each eye
- Nose
- Ears, including vestibular sense
- Mouth
- Teeth
- Liver
- Kidneys
- Sense of safety in environment
- Neck
- Shoulders
- Chest and lungs
- Blood circulation
- Blood health
- Influences on blood from medications
- Vitality and energy levels
- Emotional wellbeing
- Threats from environment
- Attitude to other animals in vicinity
- Spine
- Stomach
- Intestines
- Hips
- Bladder
- Heart
- Relationship to owner/carer
- Attitude to home environment
- Suitability of diet
- Ankles and feet
- State of mind
- Fur, feathers or scales
- Other

Reader: ___________________________ Date: ___________________

It's also possible to conduct an animal environment scan. This process can highlight causes of the animal's behaviour that exist in the surroundings. Sometimes a pet reacts to people, noises or other animals in the home. When this happens, it's possible to identify some triggers of particular behaviours.

This reading is to determine how a particular pet feels about its environment and the dynamic between this and other animals or people in the immediate surroundings. It's an opportunity to go beyond whether the animal likes or dislikes the people it lives with, to determine if it is sensitive to undercurrents, to longstanding emotions such as guilt, fear, sadness or chronic depression that might be routinely experienced by the human cohabitants. If this pet is absorbing negative feelings from the immediate surroundings, take a moment to decide what might help ease these pent-up emotions.

ANIMAL ENVIRONMENT SCAN

1. Begin by focusing on an image of the animal.
2. Expand your mental awareness to include the pet's home environment, both inside and outside.
3. Ask yourself:
    - How does this animal feel about its environment?
    - Does it enjoy a sense of safety and security? If not, why not?
    - What perceived threats are sources of tension or fear?
    - Who is the animal's primary caregiver?
    - How does the animal feel about this person?
    - If there are other important caregivers, how does the pet feel about each of these people?
    - Are there any different animals in the immediate vicinity?
    - How does it relate to any other animals living close by?
    - What, if any, are the sources of joy for the pet in its surroundings?
    - Are there any underlying causes of tension or fear where it lives?
    - Are there any longstanding issues still unresolved for this animal?

- Has this pet previously lived in other locations?
- If so, how did this pet feel about leaving previous locations? Some pets, such as cats, can take time to adjust to a new territory.
- Does this animal feel safe within its territory?
- Is there anything (diet, bedding, water, exercise, etc.) that the pet would like to change to improve the immediate surroundings?
- Is there anything else that might improve its quality of life right now?

ANIMAL COMMUNICATION MEDITATION

Sometimes it's best to directly ask the animal questions and let it communicate for itself. Forming a direct link with the animal is easier during meditation, but intuitively asking a pet some direct questions during a scanning session is more straightforward. This process often requires several attempts to refine the steps and improve the clarity of received information. Taking notes directly after each meditation enables you to review the information later to gauge its accuracy.

A more detailed meditation can be found online at **www.paulfentonsmith.com/downloads**, but for now, I'll assume that you have some familiarity with meditation. A simple method for using this meditation is to read the text below aloud and record it on your phone. Then play it back and enjoy the process.

1. Make yourself comfortable in a quiet space where you're unlikely to be disturbed by a phone, family members or pets.
2. Light a candle and play some soft, soothing music to screen out audible distractions if required.
3. Study the image of the animal you want to communicate with before starting. This process is more effective with living animals. Contacting deceased pets requires a different, more complicated procedure.

4. Close your eyes and take three deep breaths, releasing each breath slowly, almost as a sigh.
5. Become aware of your physical body, your posture and how you feel in the surroundings, then release this awareness. Notice any sounds around you and then let them go. Each time your attention is drawn to outside distractions, simply be aware of this and release them.
6. Internally, focus on a solid number '5'. In your mind, make this '5' interesting, unusual and easy to imagine. It might be assembled from smooth, white stones collected on a beach or a wide number '5' freshly mown into a tall lawn. While focusing on this '5' in your mind, allow yourself to drift gently, deeper ... away from everyday demands, and deeper within yourself.
7. Now drift deeper down to a solid number '4' in your mind. Concentrate on the image of the '4' in your mind as you drift even deeper still. Allow your neck and throat to relax while focusing on this number '4'. Your neck is still supportive but relaxed.
8. Now drift deeper, deeper down to a solid number '3'. Focus on the number '3' as you're relaxing your chest and lungs, arms, hands and fingers.
9. Drift even deeper still, gently down to a solid number '2'. As you focus your thoughts and attention on this number '2', allow the muscles of your stomach to gently unwind. Relax your abdomen, buttocks and pelvis as you float gently, deeper within yourself. Relaxing and drifting down with each and every breath.
10. Deeper down to a clear number '1'. As you focus on this solid number '1' in your mind, feel yourself drifting deeper with each and every breath you take. Allow the muscles of your thighs, calves and feet to relax, while floating deeper within yourself.
11. Down to '0' now. As you focus on the number '0', allow yourself to become calm, centred and still. Leaving behind all surface thoughts as you drift gently deeper.
12. Stretching out before you in your mind's eye is a staircase, comprising 14 steps leading down to a white door. In a moment, you'll descend this staircase and open that door. On the other side of that door is a

small sunroom, with a row of large windows, two comfortable sofas and a low table. The animal you'll be examining today is on the floor or on that table.

13. Descend the stairs now, drifting deeper with each and every step you take. The images are becoming clear and sharper in your mind as you glide deeper. Now you're standing in front of a white door.
14. Open that door now, step into the bright sunroom, with views over a lush garden. Take a seat on one of the sofas and settle in.
15. Now you're gradually becoming aware of the animal you meet with today. You'll be communicating inwardly with this animal, so mentally say, "Hello."
16. Now gently question this animal and hear its responses internally. Ask one question at a time and allow time for the animal to respond.
17. Finish this process now by internally thanking the animal and saying, "Goodbye."
18. Now retrace your steps, leaving the sunroom and ascending the staircase.
19. It's time to let this scene go now. Count from one to three in your mind, taking a deep inward breath between each number, as you bring yourself back to the surface, into the present time.
20. On the count of three, you'll be wide awake, full of energy and vitality and clearly able to recall everything from your recent meditation.
21. One, take a deep breath. You can feel yourself floating back to the surface. Two, another deep breath, coming closer now. Three, you're drifting back to conscious awareness of your surroundings. Opening your eyes, feeling wide awake, feeling refreshed, relaxed and revitalised.
22. Write down everything you have learned about this animal while the information is fresh in your mind.

10. IMPROVING QUESTIONS FOR BETTER ANSWERS

ALTHOUGH BOTH THE READER AND CLIENT BEING IN THE SAME room for a reading is the traditional, accepted method, most people simply don't have time to take an afternoon off to spend an hour with a clairvoyant. With improvements in technology, they don't need to. People consult clairvoyants in different cities, countries and time zones. Experienced intuitive practitioners have adapted personal skills to read for people far away.

Many clients know that they have the power to change the outcome of predicted events, through examining choices, making decisions or changing behaviours. They accept that what they do today shapes tomorrow.

People often want to know how past decisions and actions have influenced their current circumstances and what they can do to ensure better results from future opportunities. Most people take responsibility for outcomes, which means they are increasingly asking clairvoyants what significant choices lay ahead so that they can shape their destinies. A clairvoyant reading today is really a team effort between client and practitioner. It's a chance to examine life maps and re-plot different directions towards new goals if necessary or simply confirm current choices.

Here are some sample questions I've heard from clients recently.

- Where is my current path in life leading me?
- What obstacles can I prepare for on the path to my life goals?
- Is there a more rewarding journey for me to take in life?

- If so, how can I begin this pursuit?
- What innate skills and talents can assist me towards my goals?
- What expertise do I need to develop to move forward more smoothly?
- What unresolved issues, fears and doubts are obstructing my progress?
- Who can help me in pursuit of my deeper life purpose?
- Who is currently hindering me in my direction?
- What do I most need to know right now?
- What can I do now to lighten my burden?

These straightforward questions can be explored in meditations at home. With practice, most people improve personal intuitive skills and only require the assistance of a clairvoyant if they're unable to see current opportunities, saving money and time. It's a simple choice. Develop your intuition and use it as a life navigation instrument or consult a suitable clairvoyant when important alternatives arise. Both options have their strengths and weaknesses.

Developing natural intuitive talents requires time and repetitive effort to build effective skills and maintain them. Those moments of peace and inner stillness while practising can be calm islands of deep tranquillity in a busy life. Having well-honed intuition helps when making urgent choices. If finding a clairvoyant is the preferred option, the downside is that when important decisions are looming, it might involve a long wait for an appointment.

INACCURACIES IN PREDICTIONS

Occasionally, lower-than-expected accuracy in predictions occurs for different reasons. When a client asks about a career change and is hopeful about a specific job, it's sometimes obvious that the particular position is not likely to be offered to them. When this happens, I usually look ahead to see if another, perhaps more suitable career choice is likely to emerge, to help the client leave the session with hope.

Career was a primary focus for a friend I read for over the past year. Jasmine had been transitioning out of a job and into what she hoped might be her final career chapter. It wasn't easy, as she felt more invisible to employers since turning fifty. Instead of accepting current circumstances as her friends advised her to do, she examined her options and determined the best path forward. Enjoying a challenge, she wanted to prove that she was capable of writing her final career chapter on her own terms. She saw it as simply a project, to be managed like any other.

I read for Jasmine four times that year, watching as she tweaked her resume, networked carefully for career opportunities and delivered talks and workshops at conferences. She was aware that her next position might arrive from any direction, so she actively improved her profile in her industry. In her first reading, I switched from answering specific questions to looking ahead to glimpse opportunities for suitable jobs. I explained that an unexpected approach regarding a job offer would occur between October and December that year in a large, international company. Later in that session, I mentioned that although the interview would go well, the company was likely to withdraw but eventually return for more discussions at a later date.

In November that year, she was approached by a recruiter about a position that would double her annual salary. Jasmine was happy with the initial interview. As predicted, the recruiter phoned later to inform her that the company had decided to go in another direction.

Undeterred, several months later, Jasmine applied for a position with a smaller company but did not even make the candidate shortlist. However, several weeks later, someone from that company phoned to invite her for an interview. I wondered if I had confused these two separate jobs as one when reading for Jasmine.

Having more faith in me than I had in myself, Jasmine remained confident that the recruiters who interviewed her in November would be back in touch about that position. To check this, she researched that company's website and noticed that there was no role that matched the recruiter's description listed. Consequently, she felt that either the company had decided not to go ahead with the position or had postponed the process due to more pressing issues.

I can usually pinpoint the moment when trauma has occurred in a client's life, but I seemed unable to look ahead to see which interview resulted in a new job for Jasmine. In her next reading, I decided I'd use a tried-and-trusted method — I'd ask to be shown Jasmine at work in her new position and work backwards from there. If I described the office, the views from the window plus a few co-workers, she might recognise the environment when she arrived for her initial interview.

But descriptions of her office and work colleagues proved unhelpful because all her interviews took place on screen. It might have been more beneficial to request an intuitive image of Jasmine looking at her phone, to glimpse the date on the screen. Since then, Jasmine has been contacted by the recruiters from the November interview about another position with a different company. This occurred five days after she had accepted a new role, so she didn't pursue that particular offer. My quest for increased precision continues.

ASKING THE RIGHT QUESTIONS

Knowing the best questions to ask during a psychic reading can mean the difference between clarity or confusion. Sometimes a reader intuitively glimpses a scene that makes no sense to the client. When this occurs, it's possible to either request additional information or to move intuitive perception back in time one hour or one day to see more images and gain context. The more details provided, the easier it is for the client to identify future events when they unfold.

Occasionally, it's not possible to supply any additional background information, leaving the client to discover the significance of the prediction months or even years later. This is especially true when the client isn't really interested in what is being said, preferring to focus on urgent issues. In one reading, I described Rodney's office surroundings, and he was confused. He had applied for a new role in his current company and I intuitively saw a room that didn't resemble any inside his ultra-modern, central city glass office tower.

My description was of a 1970s-style office with wooden doors and frosted glass screens to the ceiling. His current office was open-plan with colourful desks, multiple screens and headsets. As events unfolded, his company acquired an existing business nearby that was located in a 1960s building. Rodney's job was to streamline the business while working from an office in that old building. In his next reading, Rodney reminded me about the frosted glass, before carefully instructing me to predict when he'd return to the slick office at headquarters.

RETRIEVING BACKGROUND INFORMATION TO CLARIFY INTUITIVE IMAGES

- Take time to explore every aspect, to notice the people, the surroundings or minor details that might identify the location. Look for newspaper headlines, a book title, a car number plate, the power point on a wall (these vary from country to country), a view from a window, a symbol on a car key, a wall calendar, the date on a phone screen, the destination shown on a passing tram or bus if it's an outside event (and what language it is), as these observations help establish the location, time period and type of occasion.
- If possible, intuitively move back or forward in time, an hour at first. If this doesn't help, move to an earlier moment and then forward several hours or one whole day from the scene you've intuitively glimpsed. When I saw a recent client arriving at a wedding, she was part of the bridal party. By moving forward two hours, I was able to see her at the wedding reception engrossed in conversation with a stranger who she would later marry.
- Internally request more information. Auditory people often hear an inner voice explaining the meaning of the scene. Visual readers can ask what to specifically notice in the scene glimpsed.
- Ask yourself what significance this event is likely to have on the client. It might be a life-changing decision made during the funeral service of a friend, where the client decides to quit his job and travel the world before it's too late.

- Inwardly enquire if the client needs to know more about the incident at this stage. Sometimes more information only stresses the person. This occurred with me once when a floor manager appeared beside me as I walked off set from a television interview on palmistry. She quickly asked if she'd get married. I hastily glanced at her hands and told her she was likely to marry twice. She looked horrified before explaining that she had been married just three weeks previously. I felt mortified.

WITH POWER COMES RESPONSIBILITY

It's prudent to remember that glimpsing an incident or a situation doesn't always provide a clear picture. A briefly glimpsed scene rarely allows for context. When I clairvoyantly see a situation that I'm uncertain about, I ask my guides before saying anything to the client. I enquire if it is appropriate to tell the client what I'm seeing and if my guides can give me some background so that I can help the person make sense of it. Sometimes they advise me not to say too much about a particular situation.

This occurred recently when Kyla asked about her brother Todd. She explained that he was a soft, gentle boy who never grew up emotionally. At 42, Todd was lost, drifting through life. I immediately saw issues with drugs, alcohol and gambling, plus an inability to hold on to friendships and love relationships. Kyla was the last person in Todd's life because everyone else had effectively written him off.

I inwardly asked to be shown the cause of Todd's derailment and saw a scene of Todd at around age 15 when he visited a good friend one afternoon. Carl was out but due home soon, so Todd decided to wait for him. This was a mistake because Carl's father took the opportunity to seduce Todd and at 15, Todd was ill-equipped to resist this predatory behaviour. The guilt and shame ended his friendship with Carl and led to his addictive patterns for the next few decades.

Kyla had asked about her brother but it was not appropriate to tell her exactly what had happened to him. Instead, I explained to Kyla that he'd pass away before her (due to drug issues) and meet her on the other side when she arrived. At this time, Todd might explain to her what had derailed him at 15 and why he found it impossible to get back on track with his life. I suggested that she remember the soft boy she grew up with and have compassion for her troubled adult sibling, without giving in to his unreasonable demands.

Discovering facts is not the same as finding the truth. Details need to be weighed against history and current influences. Had I met Todd as an adult, I might have also simply dismissed him as just another person with addictions, possibly with an undiagnosed personality disorder. However, by realising that he wasn't always like this and that trauma had shaped him this way, I might be more likely to explore the lost person within, tortured by the past and living with residual shame. It's important to remember that judgements about people are rarely accurate without context. A complete picture is not always available in personal readings due to time constraints.

With power comes responsibility. Telling Kyla in detail about events in Todd's early life was likely to leave her feeling overwhelmed and powerless to save her brother but maybe wanting to discuss it with Todd. It was not my position to pre-empt Todd's need for privacy about past personal issues or even acknowledge the incident. It wasn't Todd's reading. It was unlikely that Todd would want to undertake the arduous task of unravelling and healing the past and then grieving the lost years and opportunities since. Todd had received a third-class ticket in a first-world life. Had he come for a reading, my guides might have allowed me to explain more of his past to him but I was reading for his sister. Revealing more to her might be intruding into Todd's life. Energetic trespassing is best avoided. If I had spoken more freely with Kyla and she had mentioned what I had said to Todd, I'd be karmically responsible for the fallout. As Todd wasn't in the room, it was not my place to delve deeper into his life.

Clairvoyant readings appear to be simple conversations. However, during the process, experienced readers are working diligently. While giving predictions, they are also wording questions, searching for information, gauging what is appropriate to tell clients and determining what people are capable of hearing at that time. Some days it can be exhausting work.

STRENGTHENING INTUITIVE SKILLS

There are many effective ways to improve personal intuition, particularly for people who have high expectations or set firm goals to achieve when learning new skills. A diary is an important tool to record practice sessions, the name of the person you read for and the duration of the process. It is vital to list the major points from practice readings soon after concluding. It's also beneficial to follow up later to determine accuracy because this builds confidence.

When practising with volunteers or friends, record the details in an intuitive diary immediately after each reading or risk forgetting important points. Students tell me that they have forgotten up to 50 per cent of what they told a volunteer client a few hours after the session. This low retention rate is common. As a professional reader, I deliberately forget each client's details immediately afterwards, to ensure past readings do not influence me when sitting with new clients.

When reading for several consecutive volunteers, take five minutes for a cup of tea or a glass of water between sessions and use this time to write notes in your diary. There is no better way to determine personal accuracy than to record the details and look back periodically. Clients or volunteers may ask for another session (particularly if it's free) even if your previous predictions weren't correct, so a returning client is not necessarily a confirmation of precise results. Sometimes people discover a higher precision rate for financial or job predictions than for relationship forecasts. This might highlight a specialty talent or could suggest that more effort is required to improve weaker areas.

Giving predictions is the most effective way to build and refine skills because doing is learning — if you're paying attention. Real practice means going through the process for other people, face-to-face or via video or phone call, and it involves saying aloud what you sense. Predictions for yourself don't count as practice. When people read for themselves, they ignore cards they don't like, rarely say aloud what they see or sense and there isn't the tension and pressure that accompanies a paid session for a stranger. If a singer practises only in front of a bedroom mirror, they are not familiar with handling an audience when performing in public. What's missing is the stress connected to expectations. This pressure never recedes completely, even for experienced psychics. Professionals juggle the process of receiving information, deciding what they can say aloud and what needs to be filtered, assessing if the person hearing it can understand what is being said and reframing it if required. It's not unusual for clairvoyants to be mentally juggling five tasks at once during a session, while the process seems like natural conversation.

When gaining experience, if in doubt about how to proceed with a client's issue, enquire inwardly about what is important to focus on at that moment. Sometimes an underlying issue bears no resemblance to the question presented. A person enquiring about how to improve personal wealth could be afraid that their partner will leave if current financial issues are not resolved soon. This seems like a financial question but it's fundamentally about the security of an ongoing relationship.

A powerful psychic experience doesn't have to occur in a professional setting. Carlie explained that a weekend yoga retreat provided her with much-needed insight when she rested on a grassy slope outside the hall during a tea break. As she gazed down the hill at gently swaying tree tops, a woman sat down nearby, holding a steaming cup of tea.

"First time here?" she asked.

"Yes. It's so tranquil. Freezing cold but peaceful," replied Carlie. They talked for a few minutes before her acquaintance frowned, as she wrestled with what she wanted to say next.

"Please tell me if you think this is none of my business but during the last session, I sat directly behind you. As we moved through the asanas, I repeatedly sensed that you were struggling with a big decision. The words that kept swirling around in my head were, 'Tell her to take the job and enjoy the travelling.' That's it really. It rippled through my thoughts continuously for 20 minutes."

Carlie was amazed that a stranger was telling her this. Three days before the yoga retreat, she had been offered a new position. The role was a huge step up for her but it included regular interstate visits with two or three overseas trips each year. She had been struggling with accepting the new job, worried that her family might resist the changes it would bring. Her fellow student was the right person at the time to provide the information Carlie needed to move forward with her career decision. Several years later, she told me she loved her new job and was glad that she pursued the opportunity when it arrived.

11. THE POWER OF SPIRITUAL NOURISHMENT

REGULARLY TOPPING UP PERSONAL ENERGY RESERVES ENSURES you make decisions without fear, greed or desperation. If you've ever sat down to lunch in a café while famished with a friend who isn't hungry, you'll know the difference. You're quick to scan the menu, make a choice and catch the waiter's eye. You order quickly and nod to your friend, who begins with questions about whether they can order sourdough buns with the burger, what the salad contains, ingredient by ingredient, and then changes their mind four times about their drinks order. Just when you think they're finished, they compliment the waiter on their watch and they begin a discussion about retro watches and their potential to be collector classics.

At this point, you're ready to take a bite out of the table and seriously consider opening a food delivery app on your phone to see if you can have a pizza delivered while the waiter gives your friend the spelling of the name of the store where they purchased their watch. You stare enviously as food is delivered to a couple nearby, wondering if it would be rude to offer to buy the bowl of fries carefully placed between them. Physical hunger and perhaps low blood sugar levels are influencing your decisions, as you retrieve a pen from your backpack and write '*Starving!*' on your napkin. After showing your friend the napkin, you devour it ravenously.

When Jess asked about Tommy, an old school crush that she hadn't pursued, her beaming smile suggested she was ready for a new relationship. Having been married and divorced, she now lived with her 10-year-old daughter, Emma.

When high school ended, Jess moved away to another part of the country, losing contact with everyone in her social circle. Twenty-five years later, Tommy found her via social media and wanted to catch up. They began messaging each other. Tommy revealed he'd always been attracted to Jess, but didn't think she was interested. He lived interstate but visited her city once a month for business. Jess's clairvoyant reading helped her understand Tommy's motives, check if he was single and available and gauge how compatible they might be in the future.

Jess was in a good place in her life, with a successful business as a florist, a happy home with Emma, and a range of people and activities that replenished her emotionally and spiritually. Although Tommy might represent a positive opportunity, she was reluctant to uproot her home, business and Emma from their friends to relocate interstate. Jess realised she was already thriving, surrounded by good friends, and settled in a neighbourhood she'd always dreamed of living in.

Intuitively looking ahead, it seemed that Jess and Tommy could enjoy a relationship with enough space for their own individual lives. If she pursued a partnership, it was possible for her to eventually relocate to Tommy's city and start a new business. This was likely to occur as Emma began high school. When Jess asked if she'd end up living with Tommy, the answer was 'No'. Instead, she was more likely to begin relationships with two different men in separate locations, each with their own lives.

When I enquired how important autonomy and independence were to Jess, she indicated they were paramount. Because she was already emotionally and spiritually nourished by her life, Jess felt she didn't need a partner to complete her. A man who had his own life, career and commitments was likely to allow her the same freedoms. She was eager to pursue the possibility with Tommy to see where it led, while accepting that he was not necessarily her forever man. This was possible because Jess was already happy with her life and her current sources of joy. She enjoyed the benefit of taking responsibility for replenishing her personal reserves of emotional and spiritual energy. Instead of hoping someone else might make her happy, Jess found a range of viable sources of joy, allowing her to take time when choosing potential partners. Several months later during another session, Jess declared she didn't have room in her life for a live-in partner. Instead, she was growing her business through social media by making regular videos, and she planned to open a second store in a nearby town.

SPIRITUAL FULFILMENT IS PARAMOUNT

Happiness is often fleeting, whereas ongoing sources of emotional or spiritual nourishment can strengthen and sustain people for years. Fascination with personal satisfaction has supported entire industries that cater to the momentary thrill of a shiny recent purchase. The smell of leather seats in a new car or the comfortable feel of a well-made shirt or dress can provide pleasure in a fresh experience but not all sources of joy need to be novel or different. Occasionally, people discover avenues for contentment by glancing backwards to the past. Some habits, pastimes or interests suit particular periods of life and are discarded when needs change. It's increasingly difficult to be a ballet dancer or a drummer in a punk rock band when in your late sixties.

However, not every positive routine cast aside is redundant. Sometimes we can revive an old pastime as a fresh source of joy. Twenty years after Calvin sold his electric guitar because it was gathering dust, he bought an acoustic–electric one. He found a tutor and began recording himself in his home office on his phone. Playing music still topped up his emotional and spiritual energy reserves, especially after embracing his acoustic instrument that didn't require other band members. It was a perfect outlet when he had ten minutes spare or a new song piqued his interest and he wanted to play it. Tensions melted away when he heard a range of crisp, clean notes and chords.

Traditional methods for ongoing emotional and spiritual sustenance include meditation, gardening, fishing, surfing, singing, walking in nature, swimming in the sea, writing, painting, reading uplifting books or caring for animals. Most of these activities are free or don't rely on continual acquisitions. These pastimes can be adapted for modern life including writing, reading or listening to uplifting music or interesting podcasts.

The pursuit of temporary contentment is essentially a life-consuming quest. It's usually an unfulfilling devotion to fleeting rewards. For people to truly acknowledge happiness, personal experience of its opposite is necessary because joy without past sorrow or loss for comparison might become dull and routine. Unlike momentary happiness, soul fulfilment provides a deeper sense of inner peace. Enduring difficult days or weeks becomes easier when anticipating positive activities that provide joy or a sense of personal accomplishment.

For Francesca, it was her weekly art practice group each Sunday. A small group of painters sat together, often in silence for several hours, focused on capturing images on canvas. In contrast, animated conversation filled the short tea breaks as they discussed brush technique, politics and life events.

Painting subjects ranged from vases of flowers to bowls of fruit. Occasionally, they have a model to improve their portraiture skills. Sometimes, one participant, Peter, enjoyed playing pranks on the others. One afternoon he casually set up his easel in a rear corner of the room, with a cloth draped down the back of the stand. As the afternoon sun disappeared behind the trees, Peter's painting lit up.

"What are you painting?" asked Francesca.

"I've decided to capture that lamp behind the table over there today," replied Peter, without looking up from his canvas. Puzzled, Francesca wandered over to him to see how a painting of a lamp could light up the room to discover an actual lamp set into Peter's canvas. It was plugged into the wall behind him. She pondered the scene for a moment, considering an appropriate response while twirling her paintbrush.

"You've missed a brushstroke there. Can I?" asked Francesca. She took the brush from Peter's hand and began painting his face. He laughed gleefully as he snatched the brush from her hand.

People sometimes confuse happiness with contentment. The fundamental difference is that happiness usually relies on doing, having or achieving something whereas being fulfilled is a daily commitment. It involves noticing and gratefully appreciating sufficient sources of joy daily. For people who don't know what nourishes them or how to maintain positive daily or weekly habits that ensure ongoing spiritual and emotional replenishment, it's important to begin with simple steps.

Logan's initial dream was to succeed in the music industry, writing and recording songs. When this didn't eventuate, he became despondent, as nothing else seemed to provide the same levels of engagement for him. He played in a few bands but as live music venues disappeared, he realised it wasn't a viable option long term. He drifted away from his goal, securing a steady job to afford a home. Years later, when invited to join a music composition and practice group, he immediately appreciated the potential for ongoing joy. Suddenly, he was with like-minded people who shared a passion for music, were tolerant of each other's differences and supported fledgling ideas.

Logan discovered a range of composition skills simply by observing how other members fashioned ideas into songs. Brian was a great starter but could not finish writing a song. He'd arrive with a short melody that had been in his head for days. Usually, another collaborator left the session pondering how to complete that melody line and add lyrics. It was as though Brian was seeding ideas that the others could complete. For Logan, playing music was cheaper than therapy and healthier than drinking in a bar. Together, the small group provided inspiration, support and insight into the song composition process as well as camaraderie.

Several years later, they were invited to play in a local café once a month, in return for a free meal. This meant learning a range of popular songs that customers might recognise while ensuring that they included several of their own compositions throughout the afternoon. Logan thrived in these live settings, especially when observing how music enhanced the experience for diners. As a result of their live appearances, they picked up a few new members, including Jim, who joined them at the café on electric piano. He knew that Jim was a perfect fit when he spontaneously inspired everyone in the café to join him in a chorus of *Amazing Grace*. "I thought I'd walked in on a Baptist convention," declared a new arrival afterwards.

DIFFERENT SOURCES OF NOURISHMENT

Ways to replenish a personal, emotional or spiritual treasury vary according to location, season, age, physical health or current life responsibilities. Tending a garden might seem like an antidote for insomnia to a 25-year-old, whereas a 55-year-old might find an afternoon spent gardening positively therapeutic and invigorating. A 19-year-old is likely to thrill to the bone-rattling music in a local club while a 49-year-old yearns for a relaxing view from a sheltered porch, while listening to the soft strains of jazz drifting through an open window. Decade after decade, some avenues for nourishment diminish while newfound interests are embraced. A secret to remaining deeply sustained is to cultivate curiosity for new friends, interests, places and experiences. It helps with providing ongoing sustenance and can open doors to new friendships, relationships, careers and lifelong passions.

Sometimes during periods of ill health or ongoing restrictions, returning to pastimes that provided emotional sustenance in childhood is effective. When Lucas was eight years of age, he enjoyed long afternoons alone, painting and rearranging his miniature soldiers. It was a painstaking yet completely satisfying process, adding colours with a fine-tipped brush and ensuring each carefully applied line matched the images in his booklet.

In his late twenties, feeling stressed by his demanding job in IT, he tried meditation but found it frustrating. One afternoon when sitting in a café, he noticed a young boy at the next table, playing quietly with a dozen tiny toy soldiers while his mother enjoyed a phone conversation. Lucas noticed the boy's intense focus and how oblivious he was to the surroundings. He reached for his phone and searched online before purchasing three different sets of miniature soldiers with paint kits. Over the next few months, he spent at least 30 minutes each night after work, de-stressing by painting soldiers. It was a planned period of slow focus, after a day of urgent demands in his workplace. Requiring a different type of concentration from his job, painting calmed him and allowed his stress to gradually recede.

When under pressure, Lucas often arrives home to immediately resume his workload remotely. Eventually he'll take a coffee break, usually placing his cup down beside the miniature soldiers. If he examines a painted figure and decides to leave the incomplete work project until the following day, he's hooked. Within minutes of taking up a brush, he forgets about the workday chaos, with his focus on creating exacting lines and features. For Lucas, it's an absorbing, relaxing hobby, where he has control of outcomes and can review past efforts to determine how his skills are improving.

When he has too many toy soldiers, he puts aside a few good examples and donates the rest to his local charity shop. The benefit for Lucas lies not in acquiring the models, but in the process of carefully applying paint to their faces and uniforms. With each brush stroke he brings these tiny soldiers to life, while the stress of his day ebbs away. He imagines the camaraderie of these men, facing challenges together while depending on each other for survival. At the end of each painting session, he feels calm, centred and replenished, lost in the world he has created in his mind. He's often more present for the evening ahead and his partner appreciates how calm and relaxed he is. He's finally found a satisfying way to leave his job in the workplace.

Nourishing the soul for its journey through life and beyond is paramount, both for inner peace during your life and for spiritual growth beyond it. Regular emotional and spiritual replenishment helps sustain people, particularly when confronted by selfishness and unfairness in the world. It also keeps individuals focused on what's important in life, from regular replenishing practices to simple daily ways to maintain joy and purpose. How do you nourish your soul when feeling depleted?

TAKING CARE OF PHYSICAL AND SPIRITUAL NEEDS

Along the path to adulthood, personal experiences of setbacks, disappointments and unmet needs can gradually build a strong inner desire for comfort. People need a basic level of ease for a balanced life. However, craving an effortless, routine lifestyle can obscure profound, metaphysical requirements that benefit our spiritual journeys through life. When this occurs, people don't prioritise deeper personal development while pursuing materially stable lives. Instead, they focus efforts on finding comfort. Basically, it can lead to chasing wealth in response to emotional or spiritual hunger. This pursuit of ease can consume decades.

It's difficult to balance human needs with spiritual requirements. Finding this equilibrium is unique to each individual. Ted explained he had diligently pursued a career in real estate development to ensure financial stability in his old age. A patient and persistent man, he carefully planned his financial future, sacrificing to ensure he saved every available dollar. In his fifties, he sold his business and retired with a small property portfolio. This investment provided a comfortable lifestyle, allowing him to take up sailing, design and build his dream house and grow a garden with the help of a local gardener. Together, they planted an orchard of apple and pear trees, a kitchen garden and some citrus trees for winter fruit. After years of hard work and careful planning, Ted finally had time to meditate, travel overseas and attend courses in far-flung places. He also followed avenues for spiritual nourishment.

Ted chose a practical approach to spiritual development, but risked not retiring as early as planned. As he progressed from buying and renovating single homes to purchasing land and building multiple townhouses, his financial investments increased. Each project promised greater rewards but required more time and financial outlay. One serious setback might wipe out his wealth, carefully built over the previous decade. However, with each successful project, his risk diminished by using past profits to fund new projects and through improving his systems. He could also negotiate much better discounts with his regular suppliers.

It's tempting to want a bit more money until your unexpected early demise simply increases the wealth of living relatives. In myopically pursuing affluence, it's easy to forget why a particular career was chosen. However, Ted's practical application of intentions and minimal distractions along the way enabled him to fulfil his plans. He was a steady man who didn't want to commit to his spiritual path until he knew continual financial struggles wouldn't distract him.

Laura took a very different path, undertaking a career that paid less but was more closely aligned with her spiritual beliefs. After completing a range of courses, she found the courage to begin a small business, providing massage and reiki healing sessions. Her business grew steadily as she nurtured her clients, treating them like family. Often, they'd reveal a range of personal issues they faced, especially when she asked what might be causing stress in their physical bodies. She felt like a confidante and a counsellor some days, eventually realising that this was part of the service she provided.

She eventually added counselling to her range of services when she realised that the massage work was causing aches in her fingers and thumbs. By training to be a therapist and including this service, she could help clients in a way that was less physically demanding on her body. Her shoulders and arms felt less fatigued after a busy day, and she had more energy for personal pursuits and friends in the evenings. She joined a weekly meditation group and thrived, having finally found her tribe.

Periodically, Laura took part-time jobs in an office to supplement her income. When she wanted to update her car, have her website redesigned or renovate her home, she worked two days a week while compressing her private clients into the other three and a half days. To maintain her sanity, she practised yoga, walked regularly and swam in a local cove during spring and summer. These habits were helpful when she only had one and a half days off each week. During one extremely rainy summer, she gradually became gloomy, realising how much she relied on outdoor activities to preserve focus on her long-term plans. It was time to add to few more indoor pursuits to remain positive and avoid burnout with her work demands. During her next meditation group gathering, Carol, a long-term member, invited her to a Sunday lunch and this was the beginning of several new friendships.

Maintaining personal balance between physical and financial needs and spiritual nourishment is sometimes a delicate dance. It's difficult to meditate when your thoughts are focused on unpaid bills or workplace conflicts. It's easy to be consumed by the demands of a busy life, a draining job or financial pressures, until it's late in the year and you realise you didn't fulfil a New Year's resolution to join a walking group or a yoga class.

Forming new, healthy habits usually takes several months of consistent effort. During that period, it's important to have small rewards as incentives to persevere with new behaviour patterns. Forget about marathon motivation such as the spiritual benefits available after departing the physical world. For most people, the afterlife is too far off in the distance.

An example of the difficulties with delayed gratification is weight reduction. When enjoying a delicious, soft-centred chocolate, few people think about the possible long-term consequences to their physical bodies. "It's a solitary chocolate," begins the rationale, without considering the preceding individual delicacies recently consumed or the remaining soft-centred temptations lurking inside the alluring box. The pleasure of eating something sweet is immediate, whereas the long-term weight consequences are not. This distorts any motivation to abstain.

If it's difficult to postpone action regarding something as measurable and physical as body weight, what chance does the more elusive emotional and spiritual nourishment have in order of priorities? Feeding one's heart and soul won't lower personal taxes or make us more attractive to others and it won't directly help with a job promotion. Consequently, attention to soul nourishment is much more likely to be relegated further down the list of priorities.

However, deep, inner sustenance provides a lasting benefit that pursuing comfort cannot deliver; profound happiness and contentment. In periods of stillness, significant creativity is possible. New ideas, solutions to problems and inventions can percolate through the conscious mind more readily, unimpeded by worries, stress or urgent demands. There are brief, unexpected moments of tranquillity but it's possible to ensure that these periods of happiness and inner peace occur every day. Establishing positive habits or actions that nourish the mind, body and spirit helps people to move from doing to being.

During a public talk on soul mates, someone asked, "How do you know when you're with your soul mate?" She wasn't enquiring about how to measure or confirm soul mates but how one can tell if someone else is an actual soul mate.

"You feel still and present," I replied. "Any sense of hope, fear or yearning to be seen, loved or understood fades away, leaving you completely tranquil. You are satisfied, replete. You are usually in the moment with another person, without the need for words." Calm silence cloaked the crowded room.

"Please raise your hands if you've ever felt this way when in the company of someone else." Only a few hands were raised. That's what spiritual nourishment feels like — a pause in all of the striving, to be in the moment. It's an opportunity to remember that you already have everything you need. It can be a conscious, daily pause — a chance to nurture your heart and soul.

Buying a new car, a bigger home or a hair transplant often results in an immediate momentary rush of pleasure and excitement but this exhilaration quickly diminishes. Before the final payment has been made on the vehicle, apartment or mane, we begin searching for something more alluring that promises greater satisfaction. There's nothing wrong with buying new clothes, cars or toys, but when a deep-seated desire results in a full-blown collection of products or novelties, it indicates that a more profound need is probably not being addressed. Sometimes a sudden loss can awaken a person to what's truly meaningful in life.

When Ken's office encouraged staff to work from home, he was ecstatic. He'd save 15 hours of commuting each week and a snack was only steps away in his kitchen. Twelve months later, Ken was gaining weight while losing motivation to work. At first, he diligently maintained his appearance for the office but gradually he only dressed his top half — what was visible on camera for meetings. Within 10 months, his home office was cluttered, dusty and he felt fuzzy-headed.

He decided that a 15-minute walk each day during lunch might provide a welcome break from his computer screen, so he took his phone and some headphones and headed out around the neighbourhood. By week three, he'd discovered a small park a few streets away and by week five, he didn't need the phone for music. He wanted its camera instead, as he began identifying different birds and plants in his local area. He'd often arrive home with unruly hair from the wind, feeling invigorated by the recent walk. Although it was sometimes cold in the breeze, he knew that in a few minutes he'd be warm and invigorated from the effort.

Ken's lunchtime escapes gradually extended to 30 minutes, providing time to think about life instead of work issues. His daily exercise became a chance to enjoy walking in the sunshine, creative thinking and breathing fresh air. When spring arrived, he was amazed at the changes to the appearance of local streets, including the rich fragrance of wild freesias, delicate pale tones of plum blossom and rows of daffodils swaying in the breeze. None of these were visible from his home office.

While strolling around his neighbourhood, Ken knew that he needed a life strategy to maintain the balance between necessary effort and possible rewards. He realised that although hobbies and interests might be replaced as circumstances changed, sacrifices in early life sometimes provide financial freedom in later years. In retirement, some people's lives shrink and they while away hours watching TV throughout the day, hoping for visitors. Others choose to travel, making new friends and discovering interesting destinations.

Instead of simply retiring, it's possible to transition from full-time work to a part-time career in a different field, a small business, or relocate to the country to grow a dream garden. Some retirees use their free time to make films, write books or learn new languages, while others return to study to secure Master's degrees or PhDs in fields of interest. No longer constrained by job or family demands, people are discovering innovative ways to remain sharp, focused and alive to life's opportunities.

Many individuals need rewards for having to work at jobs they don't like, especially when overlooked for promotion. Sometimes a new car, pair of shoes or a long weekend away can be exactly the motivation required but mostly these are short-term solutions. They are no substitute for fundamental emotional and spiritual nourishment. If a person is inwardly hungry, new possessions, toys or holidays only temporarily distract from this profound need. These novelties don't nourish us on deeper levels. As a result, we are soon in need of a new reward for enduring a demanding job.

It's not always feasible to give up a well-paid job to pursue a creative career, especially when children depend on current income for accommodation and education. Instead, smaller variations, such as embracing new hobbies or developing beneficial habits, can provide deeper fulfilment until circumstances change. Discovering basic sustenance and finding time to pursue these activities requires planning and effort. However, the rewards for these endeavours can be life-changing. It can mean the difference between retirement years spent with people who share the same spiritual life view and encourage each other to thrive, or facing a gaping emptiness where a demanding job once was.

12. GURUS, TEACHERS AND MENTORS

GUIDANCE WITH INTUITIVE DEVELOPMENT CAN COME FROM teachers, mentors, gurus, books, courses and role models or inwardly from spiritual guides or a person's higher self. Each path has its unique strengths and weaknesses. Most people combine a few different methods for a more balanced approach.

Experienced teachers offer practical frameworks for intuitive development, ensuring that beginners don't cut corners while developing strong personal boundaries. They can also introduce new methods and techniques and help students identify personal intuitive strengths. Teachers usually assist pupils through direct learning, courses, workshops and ongoing development groups or at a distance through books or online videos. Being surrounded by fellow students provides new friendships, practice partners and exposure to different intuitive viewpoints.

Mentors can take trainees further than teachers, often in private sessions. When dealing with more advanced students, experienced advisers can help individuals recognise personal specialities, such as animal communication, pinpointing health issues, seeing how family history can shape clients' lives, etc. Regular sessions with a mentor can help seasoned clairvoyants recognise and overcome personal bias and strengthen weaker areas, including physical body and workspace energy cleansing or improving meditation skills.

Coaches are also helpful. They often set homework, recommend books or articles to read, measure progress and assist students with goal setting. Coaching sessions can include organising monthly practice readings, studying specific books or trying new techniques. Encouraging students to meditate regularly for several weeks or keep an intuitive awareness diary is also part of the brief. Coaches clarify goals, reducing plans into smaller, more manageable steps. They are often helpful when starting out as a professional reader and building any business. Someone familiar with this particular industry can recommend social media courses, guest-speaking opportunities and workplace options.

Gurus tend to focus more on spiritual progress than intuitive techniques. However, it's important to remember that the fundamental purpose of psychic development is to nourish the soul for its journey through life and beyond. Receiving help with personal spiritual evolution is a valuable experience. A guru is not necessarily a spiritual master but simply an experienced teacher.

A living master is someone who is already spiritually adept and aligned with you on your spiritual path. People meet living masters through events, teaching sessions or online. This individual might be responsible for guiding your personal spiritual development throughout this life, even if you're unaware of him or her. Some people never meet a living master in person but make contact through dreams at night, in deep personal meditation sessions or even through teachings in books or videos.

Spiritual guides offer help and support, usually through meditation. With practice, you can access them simply through inward requests for their time and attention. These guides are souls who are between physical lives, deceased friends or relatives, or occasionally a living master from a former life. Remember that guides are also constrained by their own spiritual development, so they are not infallible.

The higher self is uniquely placed to provide help and guidance because it is the spiritually evolved part of each person. The higher self is like a friend who has already watched the entire film you're currently viewing, aware of the outcome and motivated to offer guidance because a positive result benefits both parties. After having seen all of the films in the higher self's library, we begin to resemble that evolved part of ourselves. Essentially, our higher self is who we ultimately aim to become as the ongoing purpose for deeper soul development.

It's possible to access your higher self in meditation but this requires regular practice and self-discipline. Eventually, with persistence, a person can ask specific questions about life, career, relationships or any personal issues. The more contact someone has with the spiritually evolved self, the stronger the connection becomes and more information is provided about that individual's life journey. This can be an inspiring and motivating experience. It's not always easy but worthwhile rewards usually require real effort and focus. In filmmaking terms, the higher self is like an experienced director who is very familiar with the script but understands it is a guide rather than a fixed outcome.

Many people don't focus on developing and strengthening a higher-self connection, partly because it's a difficult process to achieve. Consistent communication in meditation often requires a strict diet, avoidance of alcohol and recreational drugs, regular meditation or yoga and other spiritual practices. However, once achieved, this interaction can provide accurate, personal details to smooth the path ahead in life. Valuable information provided by the spiritually evolved self can help with avoiding major life potholes that can engulf years of a life or derail a person from a path entirely.

13. THE PURPOSE OF SPIRITUAL MASTERS

A SPIRITUAL MASTER'S PURPOSE IS TO BE SPIRITUALLY AWAKE in daily life, continuously aware of the underlying direction for all humanity. Those who pursue spiritual development have a deeper drive to eventually return to their origins after death. It takes many attempts to reach the initial starting point, but souls travel further after each life of spiritual advancement. For those who remain asleep in life, they don't travel far after death and are usually trapped by their worldly desires and unfinished karma.

By guiding students towards the light or viable sources of spiritual nourishment, spiritually aware people benefit by fulfilling their own deeper purpose. Students profit by being steered towards more meaningful paths in life. Spiritual mastery takes lifetimes and includes people from every country and all walks of life, who fundamentally understand the responsibility that comes with knowledge — to share it with others.

Instructors often meditate with groups of people, encouraging them in the process while reinforcing positive habits. If five or ten people meditate or pray together, the group energy often provides a more powerful experience. After a collective meditation, it's also good to discuss experiences of personal struggles faced on individual paths towards a shared goal of self-development.

For experienced meditators, group meditations can be restrictive, as they are soon weighed down by psychic energy cords from less experienced people around them. In advanced spiritual development, more of the processes are solitary pursuits, to preserve energy and remain focused.

Beyond personal efforts, each individual has a living spiritual mentor who helps us find, and remain on, our own paths towards enlightenment. If this mentor dies before we do, we are assigned another living master who assumes responsibility for that group of individuals.

Beyond death, we have an ascended spiritual master who takes over when we die and is responsible for the second part of this journey — to get our disembodied spirit home. Together, both our living and deceased instructors assist us throughout life, in meditation, in dreams at night or through prayer — but it's necessary to find them first.

For too long, I stubbornly resisted the help of a living master. I was relieved when I saw my master speak many years ago at a group event. He explained everyone can eventually make it up the mountain, with or without a guide. The only difference is that those who have a spiritual guide travel more quickly. Soon after listening to him, I became weary of the long, solitary journey and accepted the benefits of someone equivalent to a sherpa with local knowledge.

Finding an ascended master had its own difficulties, especially as mine was head of a faith I was raised with and had already rejected. In theory, this should have made life much simpler. I first had to accept that many people who adhere to religious principles don't necessarily understand the spiritual significance of what they are doing. Being advised by righteous men who bully others is not exactly inspiring. Emotionally and spiritually damaged people are often drawn to religions, partly for the structure provided by these institutions.

It's no different for organisations centred around gurus or teachers. People arrive searching for guidance and a shared emotional experience. For the more ambitious, it's possible to gradually ascend the ranks within such organisations, gaining power and respect along the way. Although most people in these organisations are dedicated and act with humility and care, for lost individuals, these movements can promise a longed-for acceptance from others.

Eventually, I recognised that the religious people around me in childhood were simply human, struggling to follow a spiritual path. Even adults begin to squabble, compete for attention and scorn those who are burdened by circumstance when they believe that there are limited resources (spiritual light) available for the group. However, there is enough light for everyone, so sharing techniques and providing support can help a whole group of people to become spiritually nourished.

Attending a lecture by a Buddhist monk at a small venue in Sydney many years ago, I witnessed this behaviour. Several people had arrived very early and were jostling to position themselves directly in front of the speaker's platform. Within ten minutes, every seat in the back garden was taken and soon it was standing room only. Squabbling broke out when someone arrived with her own chair and tried to add it to the front row.

"I don't get it. These people are supposed to be Buddhists. Why are they fighting each other?" I muttered to a friend.

"They may be on the path, but it doesn't necessarily mean that they've taken any steps yet," she quipped.

It's the gold and silver key principle. We are each born with a pair of keys: one gold and the other silver. The gold one allows access to the outer world — the rituals, the spiritual rules, the codes of conduct and the knowledge. The silver one grants access to the spiritual experience. This key opens up awareness of the longer-term consequences of actions, to why some people stumble over opportunities while others perceive them clearly and how we are all energetically and spiritually interconnected.

The silver key opens a door to the spiritual experience — the moments of bliss and spiritual clarity that make traversing such a steep path worthwhile. Eventually, with discipline, regular practice and persistence, this key allows people permanent access to the spiritual dimensions while living in a physical world.

The choice is ours to make. We can sell off these keys to lighten our loads in life, carry them everywhere without knowing what doors they unlock, ignore them, preserve them carefully and hand them back in pristine condition when we arrive in the afterlife. Or, we can use them to access the wisdom of the afterlife before we get there. This is so much more than simple clairvoyance (clear-seeing). Almost 40 years of reading for others has taught me that seeing a most likely future doesn't actually help, if people don't know how to notice, seize and make the most of opportunities for happiness when they arrive.

LIVING A MEANINGFUL LIFE

A profound sense of calm persistence and fulfilment often results from finding and pursuing personal spiritual purpose in the physical world, while living a purposeful life. A life with meaning might involve being aware that you remain at a dreary job to raise a family and educate your children. It sometimes includes caring for elderly individuals to make their final years comfortable or simply noticing the underlying purpose of everyday life.

For some people, it's a process of discovering personal strengths and weaknesses and then using these skills to overcome shortcomings for a more balanced and fulfilling life. It all sounds simple until a few additional restrictions are included, such as time, gravity, temperature, physical and emotional hunger, the need for a home, sleep at night, distractions, ego, fear and desire.

Some individuals perceive religious writings as rule books, to be followed diligently (the gold key) while shunning those who do not adhere to every letter of these laws. They become righteous, without even considering if Jesus and Christians actually have that much in common. It's possible to see these divisions in other religions and spiritual groups, including Buddhists, Muslims, Jews, Hindus, Sikhs and Zoroastrians.

What will it take for us to realise that different religions and spiritual groups are essentially guiding people who are heading in the same direction, taking diverse paths up the same mountain? Instead, innate human competition makes some participants resort to 'us and them' thinking — we are saved and they are lost. This separatism is found in ashrams and meditation groups too, but it doesn't detract from the benefits of groups with shared approaches who try to support all participants in their spiritual development.

BENEFITS OF A COLLECTIVE AND GUIDED EXPERIENCE

Pursuing a solitary spiritual life is necessary at times but it's also a slow and sometimes lonely path. If five or ten people meditate or pray together or even donate time together for a worthy cause, the group energy provides a more powerful experience. It's also possible to share an understanding of what we struggle with on individual paths towards shared goals. Collective meditations are effective, especially when an individual struggles to focus during periods of intentional stillness or hasn't yet found a suitable technique. The team takes other participants with them on the contemplative journey. A clear group meditation usually provides a reminder of what is possible to achieve alone with practice.

It's necessary to pay attention to how you feel before, during and after a collective experience. Without supervision from a spiritual teacher or an adept meditation leader, it's possible to be drained by people unconsciously participating to collect light and spiritual energy from fellow participants. This is sometimes done with a brief conversation directly after the process. It doesn't occur often but it is important to be vigilant until familiar with the participants.

Guided meditations can also assist beginners. Many years ago, I attended a talk by a guru from India that culminated with a group meditation for around 1200 people. Using a microphone, she guided us through the process in simple steps, focusing on breathing, releasing thoughts and centring. Soothing background music set the tone and directed awareness away from people fidgeting nearby. As most of the participants were beginners, it wasn't a deep meditation. Having someone to guide us through the steps reduced any stress associated with remembering the order of the process. It helped that she had a soft, calming voice and people unfamiliar with the process could relax and go reasonably deep into meditation for their first experience. An app or a guided meditation download can replicate this process at home.

FINDING YOUR ASCENDED SPIRITUAL MASTER

Because an ascended master is responsible for getting a group spiritually home, it's worthwhile to connect with them through prayer or meditation for guidance on the best path to facilitate your afterlife journey. It's also possible to request direction and spiritual protection from a deceased spiritual mentor. This shield is much more effective than your own processes, especially if you are tired, confused or uncentred by difficult circumstances.

Spiritual development proceeds at a much quicker pace with mentoring and instruction. One place to begin this search can be through spiritual books. These might include texts on different religions, deceased spiritual leaders and mentors. By noticing what resonates deeply within, it's possible to identify your ascended spiritual teacher.

If you don't have the time or the inclination to read complicated books, a spiritual clairvoyant can help locate your living and deceased guides by tracing your channel of light, extending up from the crown of the head, to identify your connections. It's also possible for an experienced clairvoyant to use guides to identify a client's living or ascended master during a consultation. However, be cautious with this process — if the clairvoyant is incorrect, there is a risk of squandering years following someone who is not your mentor for this journey. A clairvoyant can only trace a cord as far as his or her spiritual development will allow, limiting what is available to be seen.

We usually sense when we have found a teacher that's right for us. When uncentred or frantic, sometimes we're uncertain. This can result in following a range of paths as we age, until we decide what works best for us long term.

Some years ago, a client from India asked me to identify his ascended master. This man had spent decades studying various Indian religions in depth. As I ventured into his energy channel, I was confused. There were a range of different energies and images, representing the different religious and spiritual paths he had previously explored but they seemed unrelated to each other. I felt like I had boarded a crowded bus and explained that I was unable to help him with his quest.

If unsure, I'd rather say that I don't know, than point someone towards a path that is not right for them. It can be an enormous waste of time and energy to pursue self-development dead ends.

A spiritual teacher once explained how he often identified the best path for individuals by scanning their energy fields for traditional mystical or religious symbols. If you're centred and calm during a deep meditation, you might ask within to determine your most suitable spiritual path, to identify your ascended master.

To test any information given to you by your living or deceased mentors, request a crystal-clear sign that their advice or predictions are correct within seven days. Don't look for feathers, yellow flowers or incidental signs that might be meaningless — ask for something significant. A reliable symbol might be a friend giving you a book written by or about the individual identified as your master, or you have a powerful dream involving that person and wake up in a state of grace afterwards.

When this occurs, it's as though the whole world has slowed down and you feel at complete peace. Your focus is momentarily so clear that you might not want to rush off into your day because you know that this bliss will dissipate if you do so. There's an awareness that this moment is the very best part of that day. Confirmation can also occur through reading a book by the person or about the life of that individual that deeply resonates with you.

There are many trails up a self-development mountain and the fastest route is under the guidance of masters who are responsible for guiding your spiritual welfare. Just as having a mentor in the workplace can help you navigate a more rewarding career path, finding someone who is further advanced spiritually can fast-track personal development.

One reward for deeper nourishment through positive personal habits is that it's easier to forgive and release the hurt you feel when others treat you unfairly. You can acknowledge that most of us unconsciously treat others as we have been treated. The process of nourishing your emotional and spiritual needs can also heal past scars, reducing the effects of old emotional triggers. Higher up that mountain, the views are better and climbers help each other towards the summit, forging friendships along the path.

14. FOCUSING ON SPIRITUAL LIGHT

WHEN STRAYING FROM OUR INTENDED PATHS IN LIFE, IT BECOMES more difficult to access light and deeper nourishment. As a result, standards for sustenance can gradually slip, increasing the risk of attracting entities that attach themselves and feed off fear, anger, sadness, grief or desire. Entities (life forms or demons, as some people refer to them) are like invisible leeches, draining the focus, confidence and sometimes even a person's life force from them. They feed off emotions or repetitive thoughts, particularly thinking that arouses potent feelings, including fear, guilt, anger and resentment.

Although it's difficult to stop thinking about an injustice endured, it is important to interrupt these bleak, circular, energy-creating thoughts. They produce anger and a sense of frustration. The more a person's thoughts obsess about unfair outcomes or missed opportunities, the more entities are attracted to their energy field. Like pickpockets enticed by a bulging wallet, entities are drawn to sources of negative emotional energy. Once attached, this energy system subtly encourages focus on the thoughts, resentments or desires that produce their preferred emotion. It's vital to monitor your thoughts and interrupt or redirect them when brooding becomes too habitual or obsessive.

Sometimes it's difficult to heal people with attached entities because any spiritual light diverted to them becomes quickly drained by the voracious hunger of these insistent beings. Practitioners experienced with clearing these energies usually insist on detaching or casting off any attached life forms before providing links to a source of spiritual light to heal and restore affected clients. In rare instances, a healer can channel such strong reserves of light that entities quickly retreat for self-preservation.

When someone collects a range of entities without being aware of them, this individual loses focus and eventually has less purpose in life. Gradually, imperceptibly, mental clarity, emotional buoyancy and spiritual awareness ebb away, leaving the person feeling tired and fuzzy-headed. However, before attributing this to entities, these symptoms could be temporary: the result of low blood sugar, exhaustion from poor sleep or being uncentred by recent bad news.

If, however, indicators persist and the person is emotionally and spiritually sensitive, it might be worth checking with an energy practitioner who can assess the causes and then clear that individual's energy field. Sometimes when people are naturally intuitive with wide-open energy fields, they become magnets for the dross of others. Developing better personal boundaries usually alleviates these symptoms. I've seen clients who live with partners who drink too much alcohol, who feel trapped in their partner's lifestyle choices. Personal cleansing only provides temporary relief because they are effectively clearing for two people.

Occasionally a client arrives and seems dull, like unpolished silver. I have to slow my pace of speaking because the person has trouble keeping up. I repeatedly ask if it's making sense because it's as though this person's view of the world is out of focus. When Jamie arrived for her reading, her first question was about love relationships. I described a man of medium height, in his thirties who was incredibly fit, with a small, upturned nose, blonde hair and blue eyes.

"He looks like a poster boy for the gym and probably spends every evening working out to fill his T-shirt the way he does," I explained. She shook her head, unable to recognise the person I was describing. Aware of the time limit on our session, I moved on to other questions. Towards the end of the reading, the waiting room door opened. I wasn't expecting anyone and as I stood up to see who it was, Jamie explained that her partner Chris was collecting her.

I opened my office door to invite Chris to take a seat and I recognised the man I had described earlier in the reading. I beckoned him into the room and we stood side by side, facing Jamie.

"Can you identify which of us visits the gym five days a week?" I asked her.

"Six, actually," corrected Chris.

"And which of us has a small, upturned nose, blonde hair and a youthful face?" She scrutinised both of us. Earlier, I had described her partner of 18 months and she didn't recognise him, probably because her focus was poor as a result of entities regularly depleting her.

It's not always the client who is layered in darkness. In a recent reading, Maggie asked about her two adult daughters. When I clairvoyantly tuned in to the eldest daughter, I began coughing to the point where I had to leave the table as I was choking. Slipping a lozenge into my mouth didn't help. In psychically opening up my energy field to examine her daughter, I had become intuitively sensitive to layers of entities, darkness and confusion. I moved on quickly to her second daughter and my throat settled almost immediately.

When I returned to intuitively glimpse Maggie's elder daughter, I was more alert, psychically protected and had effectively become a distant witness. My throat tightened but not into the knot it had previously.

"Do you notice how when I was giving you information about Jess, I was coughing and now that I'm talking about June, my throat is fine?" I asked her. Jess's life was full of obstacles, conflict and fear. She was pushing through life with determination and sheer will-power but beyond the struggles, it was a life of emptiness. Any emotional or spiritual nourishment that reached her was absorbed by unseen entities. I'm sure that Jess had done nothing to deserve this difficult path in life, yet she seemed so enmeshed in an urge to push through impediments, that she never stopped to wonder where her energy was actually going.

"If you can't encourage her to practise spiritual cleansing, can you get her out into nature to restore her energy?" I asked. "Does she like swimming or walking?" I enquired. Maggie explained that there was a walking path close to Jess's home that they could use twice a week. This process is slower than deep spiritual cleansing from an experienced practitioner but it's also simple, accessible and free.

There are individuals who can clear away entities by request but they are rare. Most people who do this live spiritual lives with daily prayer or meditation. Because of these positive habits, they are protected from collecting negativity from others. It's like they build invisible shields around themselves.

They usually remove entities by requesting help from their masters or other helpers in spirit to do it for them. Entities are attracted to opportunities to access energy when people are upset, angry or otherwise distracted and more open to attachment. When confronted with very strong spiritual light, they usually disappear for self-preservation. It's like a moth that is drawn to the flames of a fire that is burning hot. If the moth lands in the fire, its life expectancy is immediately reduced.

I've received this type of healing a few times and found it transformative. The effects are immediate and astounding. It's as though someone has attuned you to life and suddenly everything is in clear focus again. It's a calm, focused feeling. Any worries or concerns held before the session simply evaporate. Thinking becomes sharp without being speedy or erratic. You feel a sense of compassion for others and for yourself.

After one session, I had packed an apple for the long drive home. I took a bite and found it too sweet for me. It was an overwhelming tide of flavours, juice and sweetness I can't remember tasting before or since. It was as if I didn't need anything. I was content. While waiting at a set of traffic lights, I took a quick look into my own eyes in the rear-view mirror. I was met with a pair of deep blue eyes that almost didn't seem familiar.

A friend, Sasha, enjoys discovering people who can clear her entities. She told me once that she finds most of them in church. These are people who provide group healings to large and small crowds. She often researches them online. When she feels a person is genuine, she attends a meeting. She described feeling light, clear and focused after some of these sessions. To her, they are as relaxing as a full exercise workout without the gym.

It was sometimes a hit-or-miss approach. There were plenty of gatherings where Sasha left feeling just as she did when she arrived. After positive energy-clearing sessions, she noticed that some of her friends often called for long chats, reducing her euphoria. This was probably because they instinctively sensed that Sasha's energy field was very bright that day.

After an effective energy-clearing session, it's a great time to make a list, plan your life and make resolutions, as you're likely to make more positive decisions while feeling so clear and centred. Regular meditation and positive spiritual habits allow a person to feel clear-headed and deeply relaxed without the need for a healer. It's easy and free but requires persistence.

WEAKENING THE AURIC ENERGY FIELD

Sometimes people collect entities when their auric energy fields are weakened by alcohol or drugs (including prescribed medications). Alcohol opens up the auric energy field, leaving individuals more susceptible to psychic cords that can be unconsciously debilitating. Some serious medicines can also temporarily weaken the energy fields, so it's wise to stay home or somewhere private and safe when recovering from surgery or taking heavy painkillers.

On rare occasions, people are deliberately attacked through the use of negative magic. This can happen because of envy, jealousy or revenge for some perceived misdeed. It's not crucial how it occurs, but it is essential to find someone with experience who can clear these attachments. It's difficult for us to detach our own energy vampires because of being weakened and uncentred, through temporary loss of our spiritual and mental energy reserves. By receiving a powerful blast of white light (spiritual energy), entities dislodge themselves. They scurry away like cockroaches when a light is turned on.

After cleansing, it's essential to avoid destructive habits that allow those attachments to re-form. These include drinking alcohol excessively, taking drugs, spending time in environments that are filled with desire, such as casinos, racetracks, boxing matches or adult clubs. Entities feed off emotional energy and desires, so they tend to congregate where these insatiable longings are abundant.

Essentially, daily meditation, yoga, tai chi, prayer or other spiritual practices can provide deeper emotional and spiritual connection, reducing the need to feel alive through stimulants or adrenaline-producing activities. Finding the most suitable practices are key to the success of a person's spiritual journey through life. Simple methods include helping others, reading uplifting books and taking time for contemplation each day. If periods of reflection seem too daunting, an hour of gardening, snorkelling or fishing each week can provide time to reflect.

15. LIVING AND WORKING IN THE LIGHT

EVERYONE IS BORN WITH AN ABUNDANCE OF INNER GRACE. THIS is why most people love holding or touching new babies. Newborns provide clear reminders of what it looks and feels like to be spiritually clean and nourished. As an adult, it's possible to replenish this inner grace, through becoming more conscious of our non-physical bodies and taking time each day to restore personal energies. Meditation can nourish the emotional and spiritual bodies.

Becoming spiritually aware involves acknowledging divine aspects of your own self and nurturing these deeper needs through meditation, prayer, cleansing and personal development. Soul replenishment involves addressing the needs of a deeper part of each of us. It's the process of accepting that we are spiritual beings in temporary physical bodies.

A person can be psychic without being spiritual, just as it's possible to be spiritual without being psychic. Many monks don't provide predictions about future events, just as many clairvoyants don't consider where they will go after death. Becoming intuitive includes learning about being a witness to possible future events in your own life and in the lives of others. Being spiritual involves nourishing the soul and taking responsibility for the results of personal decisions and actions. It's also possible to be both, and when in combination, a person is usually living in the light.

WHAT IS SPIRITUAL LIGHT?

When clairvoyants mention 'the light', they are referring to divine energy that is an essential component of all life on earth. Energetic light, often in the form of the soul or essence of a person, is the life force that animates the human body. When we die, this spiritual life force separates from the physical body before the worldly body begins to decay.

If someone sinks into despair, losing the hope of a rewarding life, this divine spark weakens. Lack of physical, emotional or mental sustenance are insufficient to extinguish this spiritual life force but can deplete it. Other actions, such as taking drugs or alcohol, poor diet and lack of exercise, interrupted sleep or physical exhaustion, also drain it.

When the light is diminished, it loses its alignment with the physical body. This means that the life force might not reach down to the individual's toes or the tips of the fingers. When this happens, blood circulation is usually poor in those areas and the person is often unaware how cold these extremities become in winter weather. It's a process of gradually becoming less present in the physical body. This can cause reduced awareness of life's sources of joy.

If someone's physical body becomes misaligned with the emotional, mental and spiritual bodies, meditation alone cannot provide an effective link to divine nourishment. A combination of remedies is required.

- Practising yoga daily helps to improve awareness and connection with the physical body.
- Consulting an experienced healer can realign these different bodies.
- Meditating with a group of people can often provide sufficient energy to assist in uniting these different facets.

When helping others by giving personal readings or timely guidance, it's important to be surrounded by spiritual light. This helps diminish ego and judgemental attitudes during the interaction, often resulting in more empathy and compassion for the person receiving assistance. It's easy to criticise someone when unaware of the effects of past circumstances on current events in that person's life.

ASKING FOR THE LIGHT

Living in the light doesn't mean avoiding the physical world. It simply includes the awareness that we are all spiritual beings passing through this world. The more a person lives with spiritual awareness and insight, the greater the tolerance for others who choose different paths. It also deepens compassion for individuals who carry greater burdens.

When Marni arrived for a clairvoyant reading the day before her scheduled appointment, I was initially feeling strict about enforcing boundaries. She explained she hadn't slept in two days and didn't know what to do about her recent breakup, so I beckoned her inside. She was dishevelled, hyperalert and seemed to be exhausted from attempting to make sense of events.

I realised that in her present state, an effective reading probably wasn't the best course of action, so we sat together at my table while she collected her thoughts. In the silence, I mentally asked for spiritual light to surround us both. I felt a warm shaft of light envelop us. Marni sighed, leaning back into the chair for support. She wasn't holding herself against the world any more. Instead, she allowed a fragment of comfort into her world, in the form of the chair, a deep breath and some attention.

The spiritual light gave Marni strength and sympathy and provided me with clarity to remain centred, so that I wasn't swept up into her inner chaos. She tried to explain her argument with Dave—her seething rage and his repeated selfishness—but she was speaking in riddles and thinking in circles. I made her a cup of tea.

"He just doesn't listen. He doesn't hear me. It's like I'm invisible," she said as she gulped down her tea. "God, I needed that," she said. "I've been trying to make some decisions but I'm going nowhere. I don't know where to start."

"How does it feel to be invisible?" I asked.

She paused for a moment, as tears streamed down her cheeks.

"It's ... it's like I've ... I've been invisible for years. I feel small, feeble, forgotten."

"Small, feeble ... forgotten," I echoed. She seemed shocked at my words, then puzzled. It was as though she suddenly realised that someone was listening. Gradually, the colour returned to her face and her thinking regained some clarity.

All Marni needed was for someone to be present enough to acknowledge her and to listen while she found her own way forward. Being ignored, unacknowledged or made invisible is a corrosive experience. A quick, effective remedy is to ask for spiritual light.

By requesting the light and receiving it, one's mind slowly becomes calm. Gradually, the heart fills with light and returns to a restful state. Finally, the physical body is able to relax, to be supported by the chair and the floor beneath the chair. When divine light floods through the body, personal desires subside as more profound needs are fulfilled.

Praying is one way of requesting spiritual light. Meditation is also a method for inviting spiritual energy and acknowledging the light within. A powerful way to access spiritual nourishment is to request spiritual light for others. When this energy—or 'state of grace' as it is sometimes called—flows through someone's body, it often dissipates fear, loss, anger, grief and loneliness. Asking for this energy is often associated with religious practices, but it can also occur without any traditional church association. It's a spiritual birthright. Everyone can contact the higher realms to seek help.

CLEARING BLOCKAGES TO SPIRITUAL ENERGY

Light is the life force, a spiritual source of energy that underpins all of life. If we extinguish this energy, the human experience becomes bleak, something to be endured rather than relished. Depression, fear of change and avoidance of intimacy or connection with others can result from restricting or diminishing personal sources of light.

A recent newspaper article focused on people with depression, suggesting they might benefit from being encouraged to do more of what they love. However, chronically melancholic individuals often have difficulty making a list of the things they enjoy doing, due to feeling too lethargic or fuzzy-headed.

When we remove some or all of the blockages to the light, it's important to change personal habits and behaviours to prevent repeated disconnection in the future. If people continue living with their existing patterns, life will soon return to normal. Busy individuals might prefer a practitioner repeatedly do this work for them as it's much easier than changing their lives. Therefore, the blockage removal process becomes a regular passive recharge rather than a chance to make positive, long-term transformation. A quick replenishment is great when depleted, but these are rarely required if a person forms positive nourishing habits.

It's worthwhile to begin these personal clearing sessions by examining the benefits of being filled with spiritual light. This includes more focus on daily tasks (being more present in the moment) and long-term goals, and achieving more with less effort due to improved concentration. It increases fulfilment from everyday activities and provides a deeper sense of purpose in life. This is not a path to happiness as feeling happy is often a fleeting experience. It's a process of increasing ongoing joy, purpose and fulfilment through inward change while acknowledging deeper personal needs.

For best results, after a spiritually and emotionally nourishing meditation or period of prayer, apply your temporary focus to worthwhile goals to ensure life improves steadily. It's tempting to simply rest after meditation, to savour those moments or days of inner stillness. However, if you have creative goals or projects that also nourish you, devoting time and renewed focus to these when spiritually nourished can bring lasting rewards.

For more proactive clients, having an initial clearing session to fine-tune the process is the beginning of a life less dependent upon outside goals, people and achievements. It's an opportunity to turn personal talents into strengths while discovering a range of avenues for profound self-nourishment. Lola relied on her friend, Stacey, for most of her nourishment as she was unmotivated to learn new skills or embrace positive habits like walking, reading, meditating or preparing good food. When Stacey moved away with her partner, Lola's life gradually shrank. She drifted into a few new social groups but really wanted another friend like Stacey.

When asked what it was about Stacey that made her so positive and energetic, Lola had to ponder this for a while. It wasn't the time they spent together, as her friend seemed to be busy with a life crammed with activities. Then she realised that Stacey had a range of interests that nourished her. These included dance classes, a language course, a weekly chocolate sculpting course, a meditation group and weekend sailing adventures. Lola then decided to find her own range of interests and activities that might connect her to others as she explored and expanded her capabilities.

WORKING IN THE LIGHT

The difference between working in the light and without it includes respecting personal boundaries. Spiritually aware clairvoyants are conscious not to trespass, influence the life directions of other people or use intuitive means to gain advantage. This involves allowing clients to make their own decisions, not influencing others while seeking advantage—such as insider trading—or influencing outcomes regarding former friends or partners.

Many years ago, during a consolidation of the banking industry in Australia, two national banks were vying to purchase my local bank. I read for one of the bank tellers during this process. While intuitively looking ahead, I saw her wearing the red-and-white uniform of one of the two national banks. I described a bank office that had an unusual desk sitting out in the open in the foyer. I had physically seen that branch and told my client that she'd be working behind that desk in a nearby suburb. Several months later, I saw her in the street, wearing her red-and-white uniform.

"I'm sitting at the desk you described in your reading," she said.

Knowing which bank was likely to be the new owner might provide an opportunity to invest short term in shares in that bank, but this would be unethical (possible insider trading). It's a slippery slope. Before long, a person might be tempted to tell a client where to find his former wife, who is hiding out in witness protection. There are usually consequences for trespassing into the lives of others, both to clients and clairvoyants. If in doubt, ask within if it is wise to divulge more information about a topic to another person. It is sometimes impossible to know all the long-term consequences of guiding a person in new directions.

The simplest description of the difference between sitting down to a reading with a clairvoyant who works in the light and one who doesn't involves the inner feelings before the session commences. An intuitive who works in the light begins each consultation inwardly acknowledging that the reading is a process of discovery. The clairvoyant accepts that although there's an opportunity to glimpse scenes, people and situations, the context of these images or scenes might be scarce. A sense of humility is important when carefully merging into the energy field of the client.

A person who isn't working in the light might have an air of pride or superiority, masking fear or poor self-esteem. Both readers can give accurate predictions but the one who internally cleanses regularly is likely to tread lightly and search for strengths to overcome weaker areas without judging clients. People working in the light tend to display more compassion for others who are burdened, even when their difficulties are self-inflicted.

Sometimes a reading is like a counselling session. It's a chance to make the unconscious known. It's an opportunity to help someone see how previous personal decisions or actions have shaped events. Usually, this is done gently to avoid unsettling the person but occasionally it is necessary to be forthright, especially if making immediate changes can divert a looming problem without the luxury of time.

If the person is about to be fired from their job because of their quarrelsome nature or they have only a few weeks to resolve a longstanding issue with a parent or a friend before that person dies, a more direct approach might be advisable. This is a rare occurrence but occasionally necessary.

Harry asked about his parents' health at the end of his reading. He hadn't seen his father in almost 20 years after a bitter argument. I asked Harry if his father had a heart condition and he confirmed this. Glimpsing that his father's health was in decline, I suggested it might be time to contact him. Harry described his father as a brutal man — mean, quick, with a volatile temper and unforgiving. I decided to be more direct, explaining that Harry's father wasn't likely to see another Christmas and that it was time to make peace.

"Can you be the man that he wasn't? Can you extend your hand one last time to him before it's too late?" I asked him. He shook his head silently.

"If nothing else, you'll confirm to your mother that despite her poor choice of partner, she raised an honourable son." I worried that perhaps I'd pushed him too hard, that I'd been too stark in my depiction of events. There was nothing to be gained by forcing him beyond what he was capable of or comfortable doing. Harry phoned me later that year to say that he had made peace with his father before his recent death and was grateful for my suggestion.

SPIRITUAL LIGHT NOURISHES THE SOUL

Spiritual light is like an endless river. When we still the mind through prayer or meditation, we open a tap within from that river. It is a thin pipe, so initially only small amounts flow from this tap. The more familiar we become with the process, the wider that pipe becomes, allowing more and more spiritual nourishment to reach us. This habit strengthens us to face life's obstacles while pursuing individual spiritual purpose.

Because darkness is attracted to light, it is essential to remain centred. This requires a healthy body, a balanced diet and regular exercise. Physical experience and spiritual awareness don't have to be at different ends of a see-saw. It's possible to combine a spiritual life with a healthy, happy, practical existence.

As an individual draws down more divine light into or through the physical body, spiritual awareness increases. As a result, this person can more easily grasp the likely consequences of decisions and actions and avoid more of life's potholes. Life gradually becomes a smoother ride. The person is less distracted by gadgets, desires and pointless drama and able to focus on enjoying a meaningful existence. When people are spiritually, mentally or emotionally hungry, they are more easily distracted from life's deeper purpose. Through nourishing the soul by accessing light daily, it's possible to improve physical health by replenishing deep reserves of core energy. It requires effort and concentration at first, but as positive habits form, life becomes an experience where it's possible to thrive instead of struggling.

16. FINDING THE LIGHT IN DARK TIMES

IF A PERSON MEDITATES DAILY IN THE SAME SPOT, SUCH AS A favourite chair or on a yoga mat, a tunnel of spiritual light is eventually established in that place. This makes it easier to meditate and draw down light next time. It also provides a ready source of energy when feeling temporarily uncentred or overwhelmed by life circumstances. Sometimes after a stressful day, I don't feel like meditating. My brain is filled with plans, unfinished tasks and frustrations of the day. At these times, I distract myself while busily avoiding the process that could settle my thoughts.

Eventually, I'll sit for a few minutes, planning to resume my 'urgent work' directly afterwards. If I'm sitting where I usually meditate, my mind settles gradually and my troubles dissipate. Then I'm ready to focus, especially as I know that using a tunnel of light to dump stress or dross is going to choke up that channel, making the process more difficult. By meditating and consciously drawing down additional light into my body, I know that I'm also clearing the energy channel.

Many people perceive spiritual darkness as moments of confusion or lost hope that quickly pass. This temporary lapse of connection to light doesn't have lasting effects because normal clarity of mind soon returns. Poor recent choices can often be corrected. During these periods, options aren't clear. People lose awareness of longer-term consequences and are more likely to surround themselves with individuals who are not interested in personal development.

If you've ever felt your way around your home during a blackout, you probably relied on your memory of furniture placement while proceeding slowly to avoid injury. If you're in unfamiliar surroundings, you don't have any memory of room design and furniture for guidance. It's necessary to rely on touch or sounds to find your way. Being in the dark spiritually is like living in a blackout or in very dim light. It's easy to recognise form and objects but weak light limits awareness of colour and fine detail. During periods of darkness, it's likely that the people you associate with are also making poor choices, so they are less objective when offering advice. It's like taking investment advice from a bankrupt friend with a gambling addiction.

Although these moments of gloom might be fleeting, there is a real possibility that during a period of darkness, a poor choice could change life irrevocably. In an instant, where passion clouds reason, people sometimes make decisions or begin actions that lead to crimes, mistakes or chains of events that restrict opportunities ahead. Attempting to read a map without sufficient light limits awareness of the whole page. Moving ahead in life with deficient spiritual light can restrict focus to tiny areas at a time, narrowing the view of longer-term consequences of decisions and actions.

When Candice asked about a new man she'd recently met, it was immediately apparent that he'd derail her life if she continued their relationship. To avoid pouring cold water on her hopes for love, I suggested that she take his estranged wife to lunch. A conversation with the person who lived with Jack for years might provide insights into his behaviour. She laughed at the idea and ignored my suggestion that she keep looking for a suitable partner.

Eleven years later she returned with harrowing stories about how she had pursued Jack, had two children with him and eventually realised that he had been a very poor choice. He was a gambler, a sex addict, an erratic business owner and he had concealed the fact that he'd spent eight years in prison for armed robbery. She had a restraining order out against him and he was not permitted within 50 metres of her home.

Candice reminded me about what I had said during her initial reading and explained that she had recently taken Jack's ex-wife, Juanita, to lunch. Juanita was candid about how difficult it had been living with Jack. She then asked if he had cheated on Candice, continued gambling and if he still kept in touch with hardened criminals.

Candice was about to lose her home to the bank for Jack's business debts and didn't know how she'd support herself and her children in the coming months. It was shocking to witness how one bad decision could produce waves that rippled out into Candice's life for decades.

PEOPLE IN DARKNESS SEE FEWER OPTIONS

People in the dark frequently seek control over others, making them poor advisers and difficult to deal with. They often have hidden agendas and sketchy logic, resulting in poor outcomes and insufficient attention to plans.

Years ago, I was looking at houses to buy and I liked the look of one particular property. I phoned the real estate agent, who invited me to his office to discuss the price and terms. It was a small shop at street level on a busy road and when I arrived, he ushered me downstairs to his gloomy private office. The narrow, rickety stairs were as steep as a ladder and the tiny cellar contained a single downlight directly above his desk. I was shown to a small chair. The whole scene reminded me of being a schoolchild, in the headmaster's office. It was deliberate. He had designed the environment to make buyers feel uneasy. When uncentred, people are more malleable. I offered $10,000 over the low end of the asking price and his response was, "How can I help you to pay more for this property today?" My reaction was immediate, "Why would I want to pay more for this house?"

"To secure it," he replied coolly. He explained that he'd put my offer forward to the seller but wasn't confident that they'd accept it. I handed him a six-figure cheque as a deposit and left with a receipt.

As expected, he phoned back a few days later to tell me that my offer had been declined. I asked him to tear up my cheque and post it back to me. He avoided this option by asking me to think about it. Tired of the cat-and-mouse game he was playing, I phoned back the following day and asked his receptionist to return my cheque. He phoned again several weeks later to tell me he had a plan to help me afford that house. He invited me back to his office, presumably to resume control of the negotiation. I calmly told him I had already purchased another, more suitable home. I learned a few months later that he lost the listing and another agent sold the house for below the price I had offered. I'm glad to have purchased the house that I ended up buying, as it's away from busy traffic on a quiet street overlooking a large park.

Why are some people capable of making decisions that help them find happiness through supportive partners, meaningful work and suitable locations, while avoiding most of life's potholes? Good decisions are often the result of clear thinking, personal confidence and regular emotional and spiritual nourishment. A starving person is less likely to make sound decisions about food, much less about life. Anyone who has gone grocery shopping while hungry knows that they buy more snacks than usual when shopping while famished.

It's the same for spiritually or emotionally ravenous individuals. Profound hunger usually clouds personal judgement. By ensuring positive sources of personal nourishment, it's possible to improve outcomes through better choices. Adding personal intuition to this process provides a powerful combination when finding and choosing available options.

CHRONIC DARKNESS OBSCURES OPPORTUNITIES

If momentary spiritual blindness can cause poor decisions with painful outcomes, what happens when people endure years or decades of darkness without a glimmer of light? What becomes of people born into darkness who have no role models of a life lived with spiritual awareness? They are often weighed down with poor self-esteem, limited self-confidence and chronic undernourishment. It's not only spiritual sustenance they lack but also mental, emotional and physical nutrition.

Good judgement requires a strong source of spiritual energy. This doesn't necessarily mean a life of religious calling or one of contemplation but a life where family, friends and co-workers want you to thrive instead of attempting to tear you down or crush your spirit. An existence in the light contains kindness, respect, love, hope, generosity and shared achievements. Spiritual and emotional nourishment are valued as much as physical and mental sustenance when living in the light. It's not enough to simply thrive — people who are nourished on these deeper levels want those around them to flourish too. Living in light includes generosity, sympathy for others and a deep sense of belonging. Community includes those who live in close proximity or people scattered far and wide who share life perceptions or common interests.

During prolonged periods without spiritual and mental clarity, confidence recedes. This sometimes results in mental confusion, where circular thinking replaces analytical thought while hope fades. After a series of poor decisions, wealth is squandered, friendships abandoned and physical reserves of energy become depleted. It is as though a long, bleak winter has arrived without warning and the cold, dark days roll into each other, dispelling all memories of warm, carefree summers. Dampness seeps into your bones and you feel forever cold. For most people in these circumstances, it's not a matter of if but when they surrender to a banal life. Eventually, many people decide that hoping for light to return is more painful than accepting defeat from a relentlessly desolate reality.

When there is no light to cast shadows, making decisions becomes more instinctive than the result of thought. If a person is weary from struggling and desperately spiritually hungry, good choices that lead to positive long-term consequences diminish.

When people spend years in the dark, it's as though every fibre of their being attempts to prove that they are unlucky, worthless, hopeless or never going to succeed. In dreams at night and in their daily thoughts, they are constantly bombarded with self-criticism, doubts and the reverberating echoes of prior negative conditioning. It is difficult to escape such an avalanche of hopelessness but not impossible. It requires vigilance and tenacity to learn the art of self-appreciation, realising that you are good enough exactly as you are, regardless of human flaws. It also demands courage and faith to take steps towards a better life.

When Sandra first explained that she was unhappy in her marriage, she berated herself for expecting anyone to love her or want to be with her. Her parents treated her as their ambassador, constantly telling her to secure good grades at school and make the right friends so that she wouldn't disgrace the family. These parental expectations applied great pressure to her already hectic life.

Sandra wasn't an academic success, so her parents pushed her into a marriage and washed their hands of her. Her husband Colin continued this disrespectful treatment by repeatedly telling her she was an idiot because she didn't have a university degree and that she was a drain on him financially. When she finally came for a reading, she voiced how unhappy she was and emphasised that she didn't want a new relationship. She only wanted to leave Colin and buy a small home in the country, on the bend in a river, hoping she'd be left alone, in peace.

Her parents, having retired and in failing health, were insisting that she move to their country town, to ensure that they'd have a nurse and cleaner nearby. Sandra eventually divorced her husband and bought a small house near her parents, beginning an arduous process of cooking, cleaning and shopping for them, hoping that they'd finally love her.

She had been in the dark for so long that this seemed like the best alternative for her. When I suggested other possible options, she seemed to have trouble comprehending them. Eventually, she decided that I was also making her unhappy because I was suggesting that she could reach for more instead of settling for less. I reminded her that no strategy and limited effort rarely bring success. Her dreary old life awaited her if she didn't change. Ultimately, there would be no more exits from the desolate highway she was travelling on.

I understand what it is like to be taught not to ask for anything. I remarked aloud that it seemed unfair from where I sat. It appeared strange that although she couldn't acknowledge her own needs, her husband and her parents were allowed to demand whatever they wanted. In fact, they felt it was their democratic right to complain loudly when their requests weren't immediately met.

Persuading Sandra to challenge these unfair, irrational beliefs would be difficult until she connected with a source of spiritual light in her life. The tools to achieve this needed to be simple, portable, effective and within her control. After a lengthy discussion one afternoon, she decided that prayer would be her preferred method of receiving light. She also mentioned that she met with a few mothers from her church group once a month for breakfast, so she made an effort to meet with like-minded people every fortnight.

In the months that followed, Sandra began to discern which people wanted her to thrive from those who simply needed her to serve their own needs. She persistently made time to be with positive people and noticed how they nourished her. Gradually, she made her way into a life with solid friendships, rewarding interests and spiritual purpose. Sandra's self-transformation seemed slow, almost glacial at times. Each month she experienced slightly more spiritual light and steadily became capable of making marginally better decisions. Minimising contact with people who didn't value her contribution conserved her energy for more rewarding people and satisfying pursuits.

Eventually, she became more confident and energetic. Changing life direction can be daunting and stressful but she's happy with her progress despite its pace. Today, she's confident, calm and barely resembles that tired, shattered woman who entered my office all those years ago.

MOVING INTO THE LIGHT

There are many different ways to move from the shadowy darkness towards living in the light. Nathan was heavily immersed in lethargy at his first consultation. He was weary from trying to fathom the causes of his food intolerances, skin rashes, digestive imbalances and poor concentration throughout the average day. He slept fitfully at night and felt exhausted during the day, almost nodding off during our sessions.

"I don't get it," he snapped. "I used to be a long-distance runner when I was 18. These days, I can barely walk to the car and I'm only 28. I feel like an old man — no offence." Nathan was easily aroused to anger, even fury, when confronted with dishonesty or unfairness. He regularly forgot what we discussed in our sessions together. Occasionally when he arrived, it seemed like he was meeting me for the first time.

He admitted one day that he wasn't sure why he was there. When I asked him why he had come, he replied that my name and details were listed in his electronic diary on his phone. This lack of continuity and fragmented memory is sometimes a sign of being immersed in darkness, but it can also be a symptom of prolonged sleep disturbance and core exhaustion. No doubt the medical profession would also know of other possible reasons for his fatigue.

One afternoon, he arrived looking shattered and explained that he hadn't eaten for five hours and was famished. I offered him some fruit but he shook his head.

"Sprays and chemicals," he said. I suggested tea or coffee but he didn't drink either. In the end, I beckoned him to the kitchen and we worked our way through the pantry until he settled on some raw almonds (organic and unsprayed). The steps were small, slow and uncertain at first. I understood that every distraction from a deeper purpose he experienced when visiting was actually part of the process.

Noticing what diverted him from his purpose and becoming vigilant to catch him before he lost precious hours or days with dead-end diversions became a quest. The process of noticing how easily he was side-tracked brought him away from past issues and future worries, into the moment. All possibility for self-transformation lies in the here and now. Each instant contains the power to choose old or new paths and this potency is lost if people slide into thoughts of the past, including regret, resentment or fantasies of the future. When being truly present, opportunities become much more visible. They are more tangible, almost luminescent.

Having grown up in a family where his parents routinely distracted him from his purpose, Nathan learned to divert himself.

"What do you do when you can't sleep at night?" I asked him.

"I lie in bed feeling frustrated, working out how many hours I have left before it's too late to get any sleep before the day begins again."

"How long are you awake for on an average night?"

"Two hours usually. Sometimes four if I'm really stressed."

I suggested that he keep a pen and pad beside the bed to write when he couldn't sleep or keep his iPad close at hand. Soon I was receiving long emails from him, written in the early hours, that proved instrumental in his healing process. It was as though he was wide awake, clearly focused and at his best when he sat up in bed to write out his thoughts.

Although there were occasional nights of rambling text, this writing process sped up his productivity in face-to-face sessions immensely. One comment in particular stuck a chord:

"It's as if in the light of day, I feel dark, tired and in the shadows; while in the dark of night, I feel light, radiant even."

By carefully examining his nighttime writing together during the daytime, he began the delicate process of reconnecting his darker and lighter parts. His memory improved and he gradually began sleeping more deeply at night. A few months later he arrived wrecked. He explained that he'd arrived two hours early and slept in his car to catch up on the sleep he'd missed the previous night. It seemed as though when surrounded by physical darkness, he felt radiant light but during the daylight hours, he became more focused on his fears, doubts, exhaustion and hunger.

His notes from the nighttime writing the previous week explained he felt as though everyone and everything was toxic to him. Food, water, TV programs and even conversations with family members left him feeling suffocated with negativity.

While we sat together in silence, Nathan shut his eyes and nodded off to sleep. Soon he was slumped back into the high-backed chair, snoring softly. After another week of anxiety and turmoil, in that room, he felt safe enough to stop running and when he did pause, he became overwhelmed with exhaustion.

I drank my cold black tea in silence. The late afternoon sun gave the white roses outside the window an orange hue. They swayed gently in the breeze, crowded together in clusters across the fence. A small bird hopped from one branch to another in the lemon tree, poking its yellow beak into crevasses while searching for spiders and other bugs to eat. I glanced back at Nathan. He looked the most relaxed I had ever seen him.

Suddenly awake, he reached for his coconut water container and drank thirstily. I was aware that although he had arrived wanting to work on some major issues in his life, it was necessary to begin with smaller disturbances first. Examining them was likely to cause fewer upheavals in his life between sessions until he was stronger.

I reminded myself that eventually, light reaches even the darkest corners, if only briefly. The process for Nathan was to notice where spiritual nourishment reached him and spend more time with activities that filled him with joyful radiance, where he could be replenished and become calm and centred. By recognising the people, circumstances and activities that provided sources of spiritual nourishment, Nathan consciously chose to spend more time where he was sustained. He gradually formed more positive habits for his personal replenishment. These included joining a meditation group and a spiritual book club that held discussion evenings and annual guest speakers on various self-development topics. He also resumed surfing, took up wood carving and cycling and planned to complete some wilderness survival courses before exploring a few interstate walking trails. Nathan's not out of the woods yet, but he's moving in a positive direction. As he forms these positive habits, the process will become more natural to him. Then, the pace of growth will increase.

17. SPIRITUAL RECONNECTION AFTER A SETBACK

DESPITE NATHAN'S FRAGMENTED MEMORY AND POOR concentration, he is very persistent. Some deeply concealed part of himself wants to release the darkness and move into the light. His persistence with meditation and our sessions—despite occasional setbacks—became a lasting positive habit.

"I get moments of light but they never last," he told me. "It's like the sun comes through the clouds and before I can blink, it's gone again. Then it's hour after hour of bleak emptiness. I don't know how to hold on to that feeling."

"Can you remember a time when you experienced hours of centredness, or even a whole day in the light?" He shook his head, suddenly aware of the enormity of the task ahead, and sighed.

"Perhaps it's easier to remember that feeling instead of searching for it," I suggested. He looked at me, puzzled. I explained. "It's likely you were born surrounded by light. If you've ever been around a newborn child, you can feel it. That's why people want to hold new babies. They radiate warmth and joy and consciously or not, people are drawn to positive spiritual energy."

"How can I remember that far back. Hell, I have trouble recalling this morning some days. And don't tell me that meditation is the act of remembering."

"A part of you has recorded it clearly. You now only have to get your conscious mind to contact the part that recalls and through this memory you can spiritually reconnect."

I explained how he could request an answer while falling asleep at night. I suggested he ask to dream when he last experienced spiritual peace for hours. Then I realised he was so tired, he was already in a highly impressionable state. I took a breath and gently suggested, "Tonight, you'll dream about the first few weeks of your life and how much light flowed through you every day. As you recall these events, you'll be filled with radiant energy. You'll awaken in the morning feeling refreshed, relaxed and revitalised, with a clear memory of this dream. Write it down immediately and include as many details as you can remember."

He glanced out the window into the park. His conscious mind could be anywhere during these suggestions, because I was addressing his subconscious mind.

The following week Nathan arrived with more focus. He smiled as he sat down and told me about his vivid dreams of infancy. He was surprised at how much he enjoyed falling asleep as a very small child, if only to escape the drudgery of the household. While sleeping, he was spiritually replenished, away from his older brother and his parents, who hungered for this elusive source of nourishment.

"It was as if they played with me just to soak up my energy, like they didn't have any of their own," he said. "In one dream I was afraid of growing up in case I became like them, empty and hungry all the time. I woke up crying yesterday, realising that I've become like them. I've forgotten the light and I'm the only one in my family who is fighting to nourish myself spiritually. They treat me like I'm crazy but my parents' house is an asylum — everyone inside is mad."

We sat together in silence for a few moments, reflecting on what he had said. Then out of the blue he looked at me directly.

"You look kind today."

"Do I?"

"Yes. Different from my family, who ignore me or tolerate me."

"Can you allow this kindness to reach you?" I asked. He glanced down at the floor, pondering how to accept this goodwill.

"Yes," he replied, nodding.

"Can you let it into all of your being?"

"No, just the front half of my body."

"How does the back half of your body feel?" He clasped his hands together and frowned.

"It feels cold and heavy."

"Does it want to experience kindness?"

"Yes. It can feel it now." He appeared puzzled as he considered why he might have a split in his body.

"It seems strange," he said and trailed off. I waited and then repeated his phrase, "It seems strange ..."

"It's weird because it's as if my body is a whole collection of parts or sections that are not connected to each other. In this way, if one section is in pain or disturbed, the others don't necessarily feel it." I wondered where he had learned this specific coping mechanism.

"It's as though my whole body doesn't see the benefits of being connected," he continued. "I'm like this at work, in relationships and with friends. I see more burdens than benefits in unity." He had succinctly encapsulated being in darkness. Not only was Nathan alone, but different parts of his body were isolated despite being in the same skin. I considered how to show him some of the advantages of integration but sensed that we'd need to proceed slowly.

"How do you usually feel when you leave these sessions?" I asked.

"Most times I feel great, clear-minded. Then, over the next few days, I become fuzzy again."

"What helps you to feel clear-minded when you leave?"

"Talking to you."

"What is it about talking to me that might make you feel clear-minded?"

"I don't know. It could be what you say or that I can be honest here in this room. It's weird really. I think about the 25 urgent things I want to talk about when I drive over here each week and then we sit down and it all evaporates. None of it seems that important."

"Where else in your life can you be honest? Where can you be yourself?"

He sighed, seeming exhausted again as he glanced pensively at the floor. "Nowhere else," he mumbled softly.

"But you can be yourself here," I reminded him.

"Why? Why is that?" he asked.

"Could kindness be important today?" His face softened into a smile as he nodded.

Perhaps because he could be himself and his honesty was met with acceptance, Nathan experienced unity for a short period each week. It was time to encourage him to tentatively explore being more honest with his girlfriend and with one or two of his close friends.

People who live in the dark are often alone, ignored and undervalued. Many individuals who spend years or decades without emotional and spiritual nutrition frequently have no experience of someone taking time to inspire them. Encouragement is often required to help these people discover their particular paths in life. They regularly pursue directions where they serve others. It's as though the only times they were visible to family in childhood were when they were supporting others. This pattern of serving family members can lead to careers in customer service, social work, counselling or similar helping professions, but it doesn't address the invisibility. They tend to give generously without replenishing their personal reserves of energy, often becoming weary in the process.

It's important to consciously refuel the tank to enjoy the benefits of spiritual sustenance. Regularly refreshing personal reserves makes rebounding after setbacks easier. Inner light provides people with confidence and strength to forge ahead when difficulties arise. Learning to treat yourself kindly when others don't is a valuable tool for survival and wellbeing.

RECONNECTING WITH SPIRITUAL LIGHT

Sometimes people need assistance to reconnect with spiritual light. This help can come in different ways. When Jessica phoned to book a telephone session, it was for her friend Sabine. Sabine was completely weary and confused. She had attempted to contact me several times but had written my number down incorrectly when Jessica gave it to her.

Sabine sounded exhausted from a long struggle. She didn't believe that help was available. At first, I wasn't sure I'd be of any real help either. When we eventually spoke, she explained that she'd been under psychic attack for more than a year. Despite several spiritual cleansing sessions with a range of experienced practitioners, she was fading away from the life she had previously known. Intentional remote energetic disturbance is when someone deliberately directs negativity towards another person. This is often fuelled by jealousy, envy, greed or anger, especially when people feel that a particular individual is receiving all the available opportunities. Instead of finding personal ways forward in life, sometimes people prefer to thwart others. It's an, '*If I can't have it, then you can't either*,' attitude.

When under psychic attack, sleep disturbance is common, weakening a person's concentration and eventually the immune system, especially if poor sleeping patterns occur for prolonged periods. Gradually, the person's thinking becomes fuzzy and sleep at night is often accompanied by repetitive nightmares.

I felt hesitant about jumping in to see what was happening, aware that two people in quicksand cannot help each other. Clairvoyantly, I observed two sources of her depletion. The first was from a friend, Jo, who envied Sabine's ability to remain grateful for what life offered her, despite being poor and single but with a few good friends. Jo had deliberately chosen a path of comfort, selecting a partner who provided a good home and a steady income. Having most of her material needs taken care of, Jo was becoming bitter about Sabine's happiness. Consequently, she deliberately used black magic to weaken Sabine. This meddling only caused mild inconvenience. It's like having to carry a bag of groceries everywhere. It's not life threatening but it can be exhausting.

The second source of Sabine's depletion was much more persistent and dangerous. It was associated with a young man who lived nearby. Ethan had poor social skills, felt like an outsider and was invisible to most people around him. He developed an interest in magic, seduced by the prospect of unlimited power. He had read several books on the subject. Unaware of the consequences of his actions, Ethan tried out each technique as he read through a particular book.

He summoned some dark energy that went in search of light to feed from. It found Sabine because her spiritual light shone brightly in the immediate neighbourhood. Sabine's habit of regular meditation, a pure diet with an avoidance of alcohol and other spiritually nourishing practices meant that she had sufficient spiritual reserves of light to power this dark energy. Darkness is naturally attracted to spiritual light. Sabine needed to be more vigilant around personal protection. She believed that living away from cities, only steps from the beach would be sufficient to ensure that she was cleansed of any residual darkness or dross. Ordinarily, this is true but Ethan's meddling with forces he didn't fully understand required more thorough cleansing and protection techniques.

Previous clairvoyants had told Sabine that her friend was draining her and she became obsessed with understanding why. A simple explanation for her friend's reasoning is, *'If I can't have the light, then you can't have it either'*. It's a primitive viewpoint, considering that everyone has equal access to spiritual light. Sometimes the mind creates scarcity even when there is abundance.

Over the previous year, Sabine had become so burdened by the darkness created by Ethan that she became disillusioned by her repeated attempts to access light. She gave up prayer and rarely meditated after attempts to still her racing mind proved futile. She finally turned her back on the light. This is what her friend Jo had wanted. With Sabine struggling, Jo felt powerful by helping her. However, it was an offer of assistance from someone who was also lost at sea — not actually helpful.

It was time for Sabine to end this debilitating friendship. One way forward was for her to ask daily for light from her ascended master, so that she could nourish herself and return to good health. Jo pursued her at first, desperate to maintain an imbalanced friendship, but Sabine didn't look back.

To help with her personal practices, Sabine found a meditation group out of her area and joined them each week for their sessions. Gatherings of people in meditation help when a person is inexperienced with the process or requires strength in numbers. It's easier to meditate when surrounded by experienced people. Although she loved her small cottage with seaside access, Sabine finally accepted that she needed to move away from Ethan and the darkness he was deliberately attracting. Reluctantly, she sold her property after finding another suitable home forty-minutes-drive away.

A few months after she settled in, I heard that she was thriving in her new location. Although she had to move from the water's edge, Sabine realised that there is sometimes a price to pay for being sensitive and drawing in spiritual light daily.

When unable to find constant sources of spiritual radiance, consider a different approach. A part of every person remembers experiencing divine light. If you can consciously connect with those parts, even one memory of being spiritually nourished can help replenish you. It's as refreshing as a swim in cool water on a hot day, a deep, expansive breath of air or that momentary joy when the sun appears on a cold, wet morning, lending a sparkle to everything.

A group meditation, particularly within a suitable setting such as in a temple, an ashram or a spiritual development circle can assist. It can lift everyone in the room, even complete beginners. If you've struggled for years without success, book a spiritual healing session. This process can be hit-or-miss, but finding the right person (someone who is working in the light), provides an experience of spiritual nourishment. Afterwards, it's as though your worries have vapourised and your thinking has temporarily been reset, leaving you walking on air. For a time, your emotional and mental burdens lift, leaving you feeling focused, centred and inwardly calm.

It's best to avoid some daily routines directly after these sessions as that inner light, stillness and sense of grace is likely to dissipate soon after the healing. Instead, sit in your car or in a local park for a while and savour those brief sweet moments of stillness that follow an experience of spiritual and emotional replenishment. Inner peace, a lack of urgency and emotional balance can provide a powerful experience if you take time to acknowledge the moment. If you cannot find a healer and live near a beach, twenty minutes of snorkelling or swimming can provide an almost identical experience, without the therapeutic spiritual session. When you leave the water, it's possible to feel emotionally cleansed, mentally refreshed and physically tired while inwardly calm and still. When swimming regularly, it's easier to make better decisions due to clearer thinking and less stress.

SPIRITUAL CONNECTION IS THE SOUL'S PURPOSE

Regular meditation can provide an experience of spiritual connection and light. Instead of waiting, hoping for clouds to part for a brief, glorious moment in the sun, explore different methods to prepare for spiritual light. It's possible to draw light down into your physical body to reset yourself before, during and after times of turbulence. This helps to restore inner peace and improve sleep, as you're not carrying stress and unresolved issues to bed each night.

Regular meditation or direct connection to Spirit strengthens the body's spiritual channel. There is a river of light that runs through the body from the crown, down the spine and out through the feet. This cord of fine light following through each individual is very long, extending beyond the physical form, out into the universe. It's a profound connection to that place we came from and will eventually return to after this life. With practice, it's possible to consciously travel through the tunnel of light, out of the top of the head and off into the universe. These sojourns can occur during sleep at night or during deep meditations. Ultimately, this conduit is your path home when you pass over into the spirit world at the end of your physical life.

Some people never consciously explore their tunnel of light, using it only to step out of the physical body during sleep at night, for although the physical individual requires daily rest, the finer energy forms don't. For others, it's a path for receiving spiritual light to replenish their mental, emotional and physical bodies. People can restore themselves during daily difficult periods in life. Doing this makes them more resilient in the face of ongoing stress, setbacks or deep loss. In periods of grief, there is a tendency to turn away from support while inwardly processing recent events. If instead, a person consciously topped up personal reserves of emotional, mental and spiritual energy, the grieving process can be shorter and less scarring.

For more experienced spiritual pilgrims, it's important to clear this energetic pathway, all the way back to where you'll eventually reside after death. This ensures safe passage home when the physical body is released. Each time an individual draws light down through this channel, it's possible to feel the deep, spiritual stillness experienced between lifetimes. The final passage becomes less complicated because it's a familiar journey that has been experienced throughout life. It requires regular meditation and persistence to consciously see and feel these fine energies. Once you've experienced this, it's a chance to discover what lies beyond this physical world. It's possible to explore your surroundings by travelling across the globe and out into the universe.

The soul, the part of each person that takes the final journey through this delicate energy channel, is connected to the mind. Thinking, worrying and attempting to make sense of life mentally can easily distract the soul from its purpose, which is spiritual development. In turn, the mind is attached to emotions, which distract the soul further with desires, hopes, fears and longing for past and future opportunities. The emotional body is attached to the physical form, which requires food, sleep, income, pleasure, warmth and comfort. Without denying the needs of the physical, emotional and mental layers of an individual, it's important to pursue the soul's purpose. Spiritual progression is the underlying purpose of life.

Meditation temporarily frees an individual's mind from the other senses, whereby thinking becomes more positive, especially when directed towards spiritual rather than physical or emotional pursuits. This provides space for the nourishment of the soul, the ultimate purpose for psychic development. In brief minutes, days or weeks when a person is spiritually fed, it's possible to be in each moment while feeling more alive than ever before. Suddenly, there is a positive connection to all living beings.

Living in the physical world while remembering that it's temporary can be a tricky balancing act. It's easy to forget deeper purpose while struggling to support yourself. Being surrounded by positive people can help form good habits, including reading uplifting books, enjoying meaningful conversations and gatherings focused around spiritual development. This doesn't mean that you neglect the physical world but understand that it's part of several overlapping aspects of life.

In later life, many people become aware that one day this earthly journey will end. It's natural to be curious about what comes after this life and if it's possible to prepare for the afterlife. A suitable analogy might be school. Some individuals struggled with primary and high school circumstances but long after they left school, the lessons learned remained. These difficult years still enable them to clearly speak, write and communicate with others and to use fundamental mathematics skills to mentally work out how much can be saved if they receive a 30% discount.

The difference is that in an entire life, everyone and every circumstance can teach us valuable lessons if we are paying attention to incidental details. Even brief periods of reflection after upheaval can illuminate underlying lessons, behaviour patterns and poor choices that can be avoided in the future. Everyone has the option to acquire knowledge slowly, through personally experiencing every possible mistake in life (learning through doing) or more rapidly, by observing others or reading and studying how experts approach major challenges. Education gained only through doing can consume entire lives. It's like learning to play one song in a lifetime. As there are hundreds of new songs composed every day, why explore just one?

18. NOTICING OPPORTUNITIES EVERY DAY

SOMETIMES WITH RARE CLIENTS, I'VE NOTICED THAT PREDICTED opportunities don't always occur. In successive readings that I've given them, some situations simply didn't eventuate. This irked me, so I asked in meditation why this happens with some people.

I was told that I had not asked the obvious questions, including:

- Will this person notice an opportunity when it arrives? If not, why not?
- Does the individual feel that it's possible to pursue a particular opening when it arrives? If not, what are some of the obstacles towards progress?
- How can I best describe a specific forthcoming scenario so that the client will notice it immediately when it arrives?
- How can my client best prepare for upcoming prospects?
- Does the individual believe that positive opportunities ahead are personally available? If not, why not?
- Is the person subconsciously invested in remaining stationary in life?
- How can I better help clients make sound decisions when new options become available?
- Has the person been blocked from progressing in life through magic, childhood conditioning or unresolved trauma?
- What is the best way forward for this individual presently?
- What information about my client am I missing right now?

When initially asking some of these questions, I discovered a whole range of details I had not previously considered. One particular client, Andrea, simply didn't want another man telling her what to do. She had been on the receiving end of bossy men for 45 years and I was just one more outspoken male despatching instructions. Her response was to purse her lips, pull her dark hair back into a ponytail and steer the reading where she wanted it to go. It felt like it had become an endurance for her, instead of a chance to be heard, valued and supported in her endeavours.

To soften my approach, I asked more questions while trying to avoid certain statements. I began sentences with, "Please tell me if I'm off the mark here ..." and, "Would it be fair to say that this might be a pattern in your life?" Gradually, she thawed because she was being heard and included in the reading process. Together, we refined some of Andrea's questions, allowing her to choose exactly what she felt was most suitable. At the end of the session, she began chatting excitedly about life's possibilities. Having arrived looking exhausted, she departed, appearing more resolute and passionately focused on her plans. This was partly because I had met her where she was that day.

Another client, Libby, sat forward on the edge of her chair, anxiously fiddling with the jagged tip of her thumbnail. I sensed she was afraid I might tell her that life was as good as it could be for her. Although she had physically arrived, she was emotionally and mentally absent. Libby seemed unable to hear her reading, despite booking and paying for the session. She sat rigidly, unable to relax and allow the chair to support her, as if anticipating bad news. Noticing this, I knew to be careful not to alarm her with any off-hand statements. My guide mentioned that she's much more proactive when angry, becoming more assertive and motivated to make changes and take control of her life. I took a gentle but more direct approach, asking questions and encouraging her to notice her life patterns.

"It's strange. It feels to me that you're stuck at the moment. Does this make sense?"

"Yes," she murmured softly.

"I notice that in the past, someone has thwarted your plans and repeatedly told you not to pursue what you wanted to do. Do you recall this happening?"

"Yes." She eased into a more comfortable position on her chair and sighed. I continued.

"It was a man. No, two men. First, it was your father and then it was a partner. How did you manage to find two identical people in succession?" Libby smiled fleetingly at this, affirming silently.

"It seems that you've been very cooperative but no one has noticed. When will it be your turn to do what you want to do?" I paused briefly to give her time to ponder this question before continuing.

"Are you prepared to disappoint some people around you by choosing your own individual path in life? Not having control over your own life direction is like saving diligently to buy yourself a brand-new car and then always travelling in the passenger seat while someone else drives it. It's your car — but you have no say in determining the direction. It must be hell sometimes, pleasing others while ignoring personal needs and desires. Are you ready to risk loss of approval or even to end some established friendships to achieve possible long-term happiness?"

"I tried once but it didn't work out," she muttered, chewing on her thumbnail.

"Did you have any support from others when you tried?"

"No. Instead, they worked together to stop me when I wanted to get a new job." I knew that this was going to be difficult, as Libby needed to find the courage to step outside her comfortable but stifling life to grow. I paused, before asking a question that might plant a seed for change.

"Would it be possible for you to apply for a new position and take a better job without telling anyone?" She held her breath while considering this. "You could mention the new job in passing a few months later. Then it would be too late for anyone to talk you out of making the change. Going forward, you might plan all of your changes without telling others until you're surrounded by people who support you to pursue your goals." She looked at me as if I'd suggested that she set fire to the town hall. To soften the impending fear of anarchy, I suggested that she might have a few coaching sessions where, together, we could plan out her steps towards important goals.

In Tom's reading, it was apparent that his parents were determined to shape him in their own likeness, discouraging his creativity while forcing him into an unsuitable career. They had been so effective in thwarting him, he now unconsciously avoided most avenues for joy, creativity and emotional nourishment. He explained that after a promotion at work, he purchased a watercolour painting from a friend to hang in his new office. They studied art history together at university and Francisco painted in his studio every weekend. Tom had hoped that it might nourish him every time he saw it — instead, it was a daily reminder of a path not taken. The brilliant crimson leaves tossed in the wind beneath an autumnal sky reminded him of his own life, ebbing away towards a bleak winter, in stark contrast to the balance sheets, charts and graphs he studied daily.

As an accountant, he was in a financial position to take art classes on weekends, visit galleries and pursue his love of drawing and painting but instead, he glumly sat around his apartment, wishing he had a garden.

Tom was unable to embrace opportunities for creative fun until he carefully examined his parents' training. He had effectively learned how to stifle himself. His mum and dad simply wanted Tom to be financially secure which is a practical aim. However, they didn't carefully observe their child and wonder what might suit him. I was intuitively told during the reading process that my task that day was to plant a seed for a new chapter, so I enthusiastically dived in.

"Now that you've made yourself comfortable, paid off your home and invested well for the future, what sort of old age do you see for yourself?"

"More of the same really," he uttered glumly.

"So, let me guess. It involves 15 years of working in an office and then departure. Is there a retirement refuge for displaced work addicts? I see a home office with a desk, loaded with tax returns, financial statements plus several quarterly profit-and-loss cushions on a sofa behind you. The pale curtains rustling in the breeze have a faded balance sheet printed down them and placemats on the dining table include a variety of obscure but current tax codes. After it's all over, your headstone reads, 'Useful until the end.' Would it surprise you if one of your clients dug you up several months later with a query about a tax lodgement process?" He shuffled uncomfortably in his seat while I continued.

"Being financially comfortable is essential in life but now that you are, what's next? What brings you joy? What happened to those dreams you had when you were 15 and fell in love with the girl with a mass of dark, frizzy hair? She was so colourful, passionate and alive and yet when she showed you her paintings, you felt nauseous. Seeing them reminded you of how you loved to draw until your parents removed all of your art implements and discouraged you from asking for paintbrushes and lessons for Christmas. Did you eventually learn to dampen your own desire to be creative?" I paused for a moment.

"Is it time to do both? Are you ready to be practical and creative? It is a powerful combination. A hands-on approach to inspiration can pay for lessons and allow you to practise diligently while improving your skills. You could produce enough works to fill a gallery exhibition every couple of years. Then your retirement would look very different. An extended tax-deductible trip to Europe to visit galleries and study the masters' works or attend a sculpting workshop on a Greek island for several weeks. Your social media pages will be the envy of all your friends, while your tan deepens and you sip chilled wine at friends' exhibitions every summer to avoid our cold winters." He nodded.

"Or you could turn around from your home office desk and see your dusty, faded profit-and-loss cushions." At first, they seemed quirky or very 'Etsy' until, upon closer inspection, they revealed a steep loss for the period.

These questions can be asked by anyone who feels like they are not currently seeing or pursuing life's opportunities. Sometimes new prospects are meagre because an individual is in a personal winter, where it's time to pause and reflect rather than act. However, when a sparse period lasts too long, there may be other unseen factors at work limiting the vision of genuine possibilities. When you're in the dark, light a candle. Use the glow from that flame to increase the light in your life and vision of possible opportunities for nourishment, growth and fulfilment.

If you cannot find a suitable candle to provide illumination, meditate and become the light you need to brighten your way forward. If drawing down spiritual light is difficult, join a regular group meditation to improve personal skills and results. Sometimes people have been in the dark for so long that it's necessary to take baby steps. If a bit of hand-holding is warranted, find someone more experienced until you can meditate effectively without assistance. Sometimes we can discover effective techniques or teach ourselves new skills. Occasionally, it is necessary to search for a patient, helpful teacher. Experienced educators shorten the learning process while establishing positive habits early on. Great teachers inspire lifelong curiosity to discover new frontiers of a subject.

Although there are a finite number of opportunities in each individual's life, that total is often much higher than most people imagine. A common, crippling limitation regarding making the most of life's prospects is the inability to see chances in the first place. It's difficult to pursue a goal you can't see.

Each evening I review the day, searching for opportunities overlooked or too quickly discarded. It's a way of reminding myself that I have more openings for happiness than I actually pursue each day. Basically, it's an exercise in gratitude. Even frustrating experiences contain positive prospects when someone becomes adept at assessing situations for opportunities. Instead of attending an event with a plan of what I want to accomplish, I now arrive wondering what options will be revealed to me if I'm paying sufficient attention. On the drive home or later that evening, I reflect on the day and the opportunities therein. Sometimes a fleeting conversation or an unexpected question leads to an idea for a feature story, a public talk, filming a new video for YouTube or an online course.

Developing intuition involves noticing opportunities. When you flip the switch, constant choices about what to pursue and what to decline are suddenly much more obvious. It's like stumbling upon life's banquet and miraculously discovering a vacant dining chair and a placement card with your name on it. The polished mahogany chairs are generously upholstered with fine fabrics. A glinting array of crystal glasses and silverware leads the eye towards a magnificent display of rich, fragrant flowers. There are bowls of delicate fruits, ranging from pomegranates and grapes to sun-ripened figs and cherries. Fellow diners share your vision of opportunities and are eager to form partnerships to fulfil inspired plans. The sumptuous feast is secondary to the passionate exchange of wildly creative ideas that stimulate the brain. The more focus, the more choices are available to you. This is the first of many gatherings, containing numerous positive options. Search continuously and choose wisely.

19. NOTICING PATTERNS THAT RESTRICT YOU

INTUITIVE DEVELOPMENT THAT FOCUSES SOLELY ON PREDICTIVE skills is restrictive because forecasts alone are rarely spiritually nourishing. Giving people a list of events, conflicts and major decisions ahead doesn't help if those situations simply repeat existing struggles. Gaining insights into personal behavioural patterns and likely outcomes of current directions is much more helpful, because it empowers different, more rewarding choices.

Kyoko was still working at 73, teaching at university and writing articles. Her husband, Frank, had pre-deceased her and she felt lonely. Working from a home office and teaching remotely meant that she had minimal contact with other people. Her days became long and monotonous, gradually blurring into each other. She wanted to attempt more learning, but with four university degrees and a limited chance to apply them at her age, she decided to take a more imaginative path. She spontaneously enrolled in a creative writing course.

"I don't know if this is useful but I enjoy it. This is rewarding writing because it's not technical," she said during her session. "What's it all for? Am I wasting my time with this?" she enquired nervously. Looking ahead five years, I intuitively saw a variety of writing projects for Kyoko. I explained that she'd write some poetry that could be published in a slim compilation with seven other contributors. She confirmed that she was already writing poetry. I also saw her struggling with two books that were novels with similar themes — of hard work and determination bringing eventual rewards.

Finally, I saw a breakthrough book for her. One evening when she felt stuck with writing her novels, she impulsively began writing a family drama. It was a chance to create without emotional restraint. When writing this work, she gave herself permission to break all the rules. In life, she was cautious, measured and controlled, whereas this type of writing allowed her to vent all of her rage and frustrations through her characters. At the end of a draining week, she had her characters shouting at each other, even hurling insults without regret. Kyoko felt safe knowing that she could read it aloud but others wouldn't. It was never intended to be published.

For a laugh, she sent a few pages to fellow members of her writing course and they pressed her for the next chapters. The more outrageous and salacious the details, the stronger their demands for additional chapters. Intuitively, I saw this book could become a success and even possibly a TV series. Because of her academic background, I suggested she publish the book under another name. It would be financially rewarding, especially when it was translated into other languages and the television series was produced. What had begun as a private venting exercise had unexpectedly become the most productive part of her career. In the meantime, her fellow scribes on the writing course formed a support group and gradually became firm friends. Kyoko inadvertently inspired some of the group members to experiment with their own creative ideas, resulting in books for children, teenagers and biographies. Eventually, they'll meet at Kyoko's home once a year for a weekend to discuss creative projects, gossip and spend time with their writing tribe.

Psychic development without spiritual awareness and focus on personal progress often results in giving predictions without insight. This is unlikely to encourage people to recognise negative patterns of behaviour that produce unwanted results. It becomes simple fortune telling, where clients have no power to shape their destinies. It's vital to remember that each decision made or avoided, every choice and action, influences the future. If I decide to make a cake but forget to include a raising agent in the mix, I'll produce a large, round biscuit. If even one important step is missing from a plan, desired outcomes are often derailed. When this happens, it's beneficial to review the steps taken to determine better processes next time.

Sometimes a predictive reading without any real insights as to underlying causes of actions or repetitive behaviours is simply a list of likely future events. A session that takes a spiritual perspective is usually more multi-dimensional than that. Spiritually significant insights can be discovered while pursuing physical goals and sometimes, a range of personal strengths are developed for future objectives. When Chloe was young, she realised that to successfully complete high school and secure a place at university, she had to help establish some practical systems in her parents' chaotic lives. Her father had lost a small business and was drinking heavily while her mother had begun an affair with a neighbour. Chloe realised that if they separated, she'd probably have to leave her current school and start anew somewhere far away.

Throughout the next five years, she coached her dad into a new career and supported her mother to train as a nurse, with a goal of becoming financially independent. She was so effective in meeting the demands of her parents that she studied nursing, too. During her reading, I noticed how life events had shaped her career, forcing her towards a vocation that she was skilled for but one that simply extended her family role as a teenager. I enquired about her dream job. She didn't have a clue but knew that nursing was a constant drain on her physically and emotionally.

I pointed out that she was resourceful, organised and capable of juggling a range of demands effectively. Adding a course of study to her current life was possible if she discovered what she wanted to pursue in her career. She had honed her organisational skills managing her feckless parents, suiting her to project management or similar roles. I asked what she wanted from a career.

"To feel like I'm making a difference," she replied softly. I set her some homework — to list a range of vocations that she felt made a difference to others and then cross off any that were unsuitable. She could even become an intern in these roles to gauge what they involved daily. While she considered this, I scanned ahead through the next 12 years to discover what career direction she'd choose beyond nursing.

"I worked in aged care for a few years."

"Did that suit you?"

"Not really."

"Let me guess. It reminded you of living with mum and dad. A group of elderly people in need of some responsible adults and enough staff to meet their daily needs. Of course, both staff and strategic thinkers were in short supply so you were spread very thin."

"That's about it."

Looking ahead revealed that Chloe's underlying persistence and adaptability would be fundamental in her long-term career. I saw her becoming an advocate for aged care in ten years, researching and writing submissions for government inquiries into the need of retirees and aged-care facilities. Her role involved travelling across the state to assess retirement homes. Instead of reporting disorganised venues, she often helped them make clear plans to improve their environments to receive necessary accreditation. Chloe focused on desired outcomes instead of blame. She soon developed a reputation for being fair, making her invaluable as a spokesperson for the industry when statewide guidelines were being revised. Instead of assisting a dozen elderly people in a single understaffed venue, she improved the lives of thousands by being their voice to the government. Not only was she making a difference, Chloe could also see the results when she spoke with residents while inspecting aged-care homes during assessments.

Often, it's difficult to accurately assess an underlying spiritual lesson until a physical goal is achieved. During Chloe's session, I was able to scan ahead and reveal that her nursing training wasn't wasted. Dealing effectively with her crazy parents was also training for taking a rational approach to asking the state government to increase funding and governance for a growing sector of the population. She was becoming the positive mentor, guide and coach that she lacked in her own teenage years.

Imagine filling a small backpack for a five-day journey on foot when you don't understand the nature of the expedition or the terrain. It's unlikely that you'd pack what is necessary for the trip. If, instead, there are clear instructions about what to expect on the pilgrimage, along with the physical and emotional challenges ahead, you're more likely to pack accordingly. Traversing sand dunes in the desert is vastly different from trekking through snowy mountains.

Intuitive development that focuses entirely on future events is like a backpack that has been filled for a particular physical journey. Psychic development that is pursued with an awareness of spiritual growth is like a rucksack that has been more thoughtfully packed. This haversack contains spiritual cleansing techniques for those days when energetic burdens become overwhelming. Without rigorous cleansing, there is a risk of becoming fuzzy-headed at times. This bag contains tools to glimpse acute traumas that have shaped people, allowing empathy and compassion for those who are limping through life through no fault of their own. These aids build resilience. They are necessary when clients blame psychics or counsellors for not fixing their problems, giving in to their demands or for simply being human.

This bag contains reminders that we are each on unique paths in life. Some people are on track to master life's lessons while others are camped beside the path, refusing to take one more step. Many have wandered away from the route, unaware of the journey and distracted by the process of making themselves physically comfortable. They eat more, buy more and crave something deeply nourishing without understanding what this is.

When I studied with a spiritual teacher in the UK, she explained, "You've taken this predictive path in a previous lifetime. It's easy for you this time but it's not your purpose. It will not fulfil you long term. This lifetime is about spiritual development for you, so don't become lost in symbols, techniques and psychic methods. Do what you've come to do. The clock is ticking." It was time to readjust my sights, to go beyond predictions to discover why some people are spiritually awake in life and why others are asleep.

Over the years, I've accepted that the tarot is great for answering life's questions and clarifying confusing situations. However, in itself, it does not provide a path back to the source of life. It's not a way home to Spirit after this life concludes. Intuitively reading for others provided many opportunities to witness how people struggle to balance the demands of a physical life with the deeper needs for spiritual nourishment and development. There's no single way to find the perfect balance between physical and spiritual needs. It's like walking a tightrope

— a slow journey that requires constant readjustment and reassessment just to remain upright.

Each person is unique. Although lives have distinct themes, friends, work colleagues and family members often provide an array of different demands and opportunities. In the process of mastering tightrope walking, we fall repeatedly. If we land gracefully, we can climb again and repeat the process. After an awkward touchdown, healing might require a long wait before another attempt.

Studying avenues for spiritual growth with Christine in the UK was sometimes a struggle. I was transfixed with developing and honing my predictive skills, while Christine repeatedly attempted to shift my gaze to more spiritual matters. Between meditations in her cosy flat, we sipped tea while discussing some weighty matters.

"Predictions can help with this life but what about afterwards," she said. "Spiritual development is about nourishing and strengthening ourselves for the expedition that continues after we die. For this journey, it is necessary to connect with our calling master. This is someone who has passed through the world in human form and has mastered spiritual lessons."

She explained that a short list of calling or ascended masters included Buddha, Jesus, Muhammad, Moses and many more. She revealed that she had originally agreed to teach me because she could see that we both shared the same living and ascended masters.

A living master is a spiritually adept person—currently alive—who can guide others towards positive self-development practices in this lifetime. There are thousands of these individuals alive at any one time. If a spiritual master dies, another master usually replaces that person and assumes responsibility for their disciples.

Christine explained I needed to move beyond mere predictions and notice deeper spiritual issues underlying people's lives. Being young and ambitious at the time, I ignored this sage advice.

"Predictions won't be enough for you, eventually. You'll feel unheard by your clients, especially the people who want to be told about better lives that don't require any personal effort."

Many years later, I realised Christine was right. Instead of leaving this field and searching for a more suitable vocation, I decided to find more meaning in the work I was already doing. This desire for increased accuracy eventually became a quest for deeper spiritual nourishment rather than mere psychic exploration. Recently, I designed an 'opportunities reading'. In these sessions, I examine the person's past for openings taken, ignored or refused and some of the consequences of these decisions. Then it's important to look ahead, highlighting positive breaks and worthwhile options approaching. These are often brief positive moments, where choices are fleetingly available. Making clients aware of the consequences of past choices and approaching positive prospects is a glimpse of karma in a nutshell.

In my psychic practice, I've explored contributing factors to a lack of spiritual nourishment with clients. Consequently, my work is maturing into a more spiritual experience. I've become more tolerant of people who have wandered away from the light because I know from personal experience how easily this is done. I realise, too, how difficult it is to make effective decisions when spiritually undernourished. There is neither brightness nor shadows to compare alternatives. Sometimes people experience moments or months of gloom. There are also rare individuals who spend decades or entire lifetimes in spiritual darkness. Turning these lives around requires surrender to larger forces at work in the universe, which isn't easy when a person has spent years clinging to those few skills or techniques that provide minimal emotional or spiritual sustenance.

Christine was very strict about not providing actual spiritual healing to others. She explained that each time a practitioner places hands on another person, a psychic cord is formed. The more healing sessions attended, the stronger those cords become. When clients feel stressed or worried, they unconsciously tug on those cords to the healer and drain that person. This leaves limited reserves for the therapist's own spiritual needs. It is also unnecessary, because clients can find their own sources of spiritual light. Christine explained that without an awareness of life's bigger picture, it's not possible to know if the process of healing other people is helping or hindering them, especially if it delays important spiritual lessons.

I witnessed this first-hand when I returned to Australia after my education with Christine. Counselling clients who were unable or unwilling to do the work necessary to heal often left energetic parts of themselves in my office. It was like running a daycare centre for abandoned aspects of patrons. It was distracting to read for people with energetic parts of previous clients gathered around in the room. Soon, my consulting room was crammed with this stale, residual energy and client bookings slowed to a crawl. There was no room for anyone else in the space. Recognising the underlying cause meant that it was time for a fresh approach. I became scrupulous about psychic cleansing and ceased providing spiritual healing. It was time to discontinue this work and focus more on counselling and clairvoyance. This hands-off approach might not suit everyone but for me, it was important.

By addressing energetic imbalances and helping people find suitable sources of spiritual and emotional sustenance, my work evolved. Sometimes I remind clients about deeper, spiritual purpose and nudge them towards attending to those needs. This method doesn't undermine personal free will but allows each individual to identify suitable sources of deeper nourishment.

In a recent tarot/clairvoyance reading, Tracy asked me what she needed to do to turn her life around. I asked inwardly and was clearly told, "She needs to pray." Unsure about blurting this out without sounding like a zealous preacher, I tentatively asked if she prayed or meditated.

"I meditate," she replied. "I used to pray but when life got really bad, I turned my back on God and gave up."

"Thinking back to before things got bad, what did you derive from prayer? How did praying make you feel?" I asked. She thought about this for a moment before speaking. "I felt safe, held."

"Does meditation leave you feeling safe or held?"

"Sometimes."

"Could you combine prayer and meditation as twin sources of nourishment for a while?"

She agreed to try setting aside some time each day for prayer and for meditation. I then felt confident enough to tell her I had been told she needed to pray.

Prayer is only one of many sources of spiritual nourishment. It's essential to try a range of different avenues for replenishment to discover what suits you personally. Sometimes it's necessary for individuals to become centred within themselves before spiritual sustenance is effective. Techniques for centring include:

- The **'I am aware of …'** exercise. This involves stating aloud what you are aware of, within and around yourself for several minutes. It's a way of grounding yourself in the present moment.
- A short meditation to still the mind and release daily demands.
- Physical exercise for 10 to 15 minutes releases stress and allows the body to relax.
- A yoga session can help with the centring process and bring people into the present moment.
- A short walk in nature, surfing, hang-gliding, snorkelling, rowing, fishing, cycling, tai chi, gardening, dancing, mindful exercise or rock climbing. Walking over difficult terrain or up steep inclines brings focus into the moment while releasing tension.
- Listening to harmonious sounds such as waves breaking on a shoreline, birds singing or the rustle of leaves in a gentle breeze. From tuneful wind-chimes to musical instruments, listening to melodious sounds can promote peace within the physical body.
- Reading spiritually uplifting passages from a book can inspire inner stillness and awareness of the joys of the moment.
- Ten minutes of gardening is often sufficient to bring a person into the present moment.

EDITING DETAILS WHEN GIVING PREDICTIONS

When first improving personal intuition, it's tempting to reveal everything you see and feel. Some psychics insist they are only given information that needs to be shared but voicing everything received is risky. When I'm intuitively told something that might cause a client pain or doubt, I usually ask if it's okay to divulge this information. If so, I then enquire how best to discuss these details. If not, I take a moment to see how this new guidance relates to the issues or questions the client is focused on.

In a recent reading, the cards indicated Courtney would leave her job within four weeks. She's a warm, sensitive person, easily frightened and anxious. In previous readings, she had told me she enjoyed working for her current boss because he was kind to her. The card layout also indicated that she might move house soon after leaving her job. I was reluctant to begin with news of so much upheaval, so I began with a question.

"How are things at work for you right now?"

"It's quiet," she replied, anxiously fiddling with a sheet of paper containing her questions. "We've lost a couple of big contracts and there's no role for me at the moment." She paused, held her breath and scrutinised my face for possible bad news.

I immediately knew that it was safe to tell her what I saw clairvoyantly. I received an email several weeks later to say that she had been laid off a few days after her reading. She left Sydney, returning to the sanctuary of her parents' home interstate to consider her options. Time in the country provided Courtney with a chance to reflect on the next chapter of her life. It also helped her to choose a new vocation. She later returned to the city to work part-time while studying to become a physiotherapist. I'm sure she'll build a client base very quickly in her new profession, as her natural warmth and compassion for others will complement her training. Just because you intuitively see future events, doesn't mean that it's the right time to tell clients everything glimpsed. If in doubt, ask inwardly for permission to reveal what you glimpsed. Sometimes I'll ask for the best approach to reveal details in a way that's less confronting for the client.

When Davina asked about her marriage, she was weary from sharing a home with someone who seemed emotionally stuck. She paused briefly, before explaining how she was considering leaving Geoff but nervous about living alone and being single at 60.

"I feel invisible at home and I've never been so lonely," she uttered dejectedly. "All he does is work, eat and sleep. We never go anywhere together. My weekly excursions include a grocery trip, a stop at the chemist for his medications and afternoon tea with my mother. Conversation is limited as she's as deaf as a post these days." She was facing a life-changing decision, the outcome of which might liberate her or diminish her life even further.

I was intuitively told that Geoff was ill and would pass away unexpectedly within six months, so she didn't have to make that choice immediately. I clarified that it wasn't wise to tell her this, so I presented it differently.

"What's Geoff like as a travelling companion?" I asked.

"Actually, he's not bad. Getting him away from his frustrating job isn't easy but during our last trip five years ago, he began to smile again. It was like it used to be with us. We laughed and enjoyed each day. I think that his job makes him angry and frustrated."

"Can you plan a trip together in the next month or so? It might be a chance to have one last positive experience together before moving on. It might also give him an opportunity to rethink his career and how it leaves him feeling. Just a thought."

Davina completed a trip with Geoff to the UK, where she was able to explore her ancestral hometown. She promised herself that she'd revisit every year or two as she loved the feel of the place. Despite unpredictable weather, they walked each day, exploring their surroundings. At one point she considered what their relationship might look like if Geoff retired and they moved abroad. He was out of breath after their daily walks but as he was deskbound at work every day, she thought nothing of it.

A year later Davina returned for a reading, explaining that Geoff had died suddenly from an undiagnosed heart condition. Their final holiday together made this loss more painful because she had glimpsed a lighter, warmer side of her husband when away from his workplace. Eventually, she realised their UK visit was a great final memory for Geoff and a better ending for their relationship than a prolonged legal process. She explained she was finally ready to sell the house and start afresh. Although Davina was still processing her grief, she accepted that remaining with Geoff and enjoying their last voyage together meant that she felt less guilt than if she'd abandoned him at the lowest point in his life.

20. NOTICING INVISIBLE OPPORTUNITIES

MOST POWER EXISTS IN THE CURRENT INSTANT. IT'S IN THE present that a person can forgive and release the past, map out steps to future goals or simply savour the joys of the moment. Making the most of today lies in knowing what's important. When a person is centred, calm and focused, decisions made in the present are usually more positive for the longer-term.

What if you could unearth what you most need to know right now? What if it was possible to discover what seeds to plant today to enjoy a more rewarding tomorrow? One powerful key to exploring what is immediately important is through personal intuition. A part of you already knows what decisions, plans and actions are likely to support your deeper purpose in life. Sometimes it's difficult to still the mind and dispel the incessant need for constant action and stimulation, to be able to see, hear and feel the best direction to choose right now. Some people have a habit of keeping busy with insignificant demands at the cost of actions that would fulfil their deeper purpose.

Opportunities are like buses. After a famine, there is a feast. Suddenly, several buses arrive at once but not every vehicle is going where you want to go. Take the wrong one and you might end up lost. Miss the right one and you're going nowhere. If you're well prepared for a new prospect, you're at the head of the queue for a bus to your desired destination. There is still a risk that you'll alight the bus too early to reach your goal but even if this occurs, you'll have mastered new skills that can be useful when pursuing another aim. If you never leave home, you might not even see the range of buses that make these journeys possible.

I changed my daily approach from looking at my future opportunities, to reviewing recent options ignored. It became a simple daily exercise. At the end of each day, I spent five to ten minutes reflecting on promising prospects that surfaced during the day. At first it was difficult because opportunities don't always appear as a warm phone call or email invitation to an event, a request to appear on a TV program, or even an obvious positive opening. Sometimes they arrive as frustrations, obstacles or as someone declining a request. Occasionally, they present as a last-minute client cancellation, making room for piano practice or giving a public talk without notes, providing a chance to engage with the room while allowing a question-and-answer session to focus on particular interests of the audience.

Sometimes it is necessary to ask, "What is the opportunity in this situation?" Recently I was invited to submit several 10-minute videos for a website and teaching platform. They paid a flat fee for use of the videos. I made a short list, scripted the text and sourced some still images and stock video footage and put together three video plans. I prepared a budget and found some possible videographers/editors. I didn't want to spend up to 24 months learning video editing skills so I paid a professional to do it for me.

Then I checked with the organisation if I could use my videos elsewhere after they had an exclusive use period and they refused. They wanted world rights in perpetuity for each video. I considered my time spent and the cost to produce each film and concluded that I'd lose $200 per video and around ten hours of my time in scripting, editing, planning and building skills with a teleprompter. I didn't want to give away unique ideas and lose money, so I abandoned the project. It was disappointing, especially after having already devoted around 50 hours of work to the process. At the end of a tiring day, I sat up in bed and asked myself, "What is the opportunity in this situation?" I continued to ask this question three days in a row before the answer finally came to me.

Consequently, I decided to make the videos for myself and offer them free on YouTube. Costs could come from my annual marketing budget and in the long term, I'd be training for longer, improved videos focused around online courses. Eventually, I might provide distance courses that are complete digital downloads, including an eBook, e-workbook, PDF posters and lesson videos. The obvious is not always apparent. I was prepared to ask about the underlying opportunity in this situation for ten days in a row if required.

This time, the opportunity wasn't putting the videos on the other person's website but kick-starting the process of moving towards digital teaching. These videos can be produced much more quickly than books and can reach an immediate and wider audience. I might still produce some short films for that teaching platform, just not the three that I originally scripted.

Two days before the videographer was due to begin filming, Sydney went into a COVID-19 pandemic lockdown and the shoot was postponed. Three months passed before I was able to film the videos. The delay was frustrating, so again I asked, "What is the opportunity in this for me?" This time the answer was simple.

The videographer had suggested that I download some teleprompter software and practise using it before the filming day. Instead of glancing down at my notes, I could simply read on a screen what I had written, while filming. I followed his advice and realised how awkward I was at first. After tweaking the speed of the text and working on my tendency to touch my face and wave my hands around while speaking, I began to improve. By the time the recording day arrived, I was confident with the process and ready to take direction from the videographer who was viewing the content on screen in real time.

Had we filmed these videos before practising with the teleprompter software, I'd probably have uploaded them to YouTube and then removed them a few months later, after gaining more experience with the process. This irritating delay allowed me to refine my skills before the first video was even recorded. It saved time and money plus the cringe factor of seeing an incompetent first attempt. Initial efforts on new projects often need to be refined and practising a process until you're confident and familiar with it usually shows in the finished result. I realised that sometimes, a delay or having to abandon plans completely can lead to more positive outcomes.

21. USING CLAIRVOYANCE TO NOTICE OPPORTUNITIES

PSYCHOLOGIST SELENA WAS EXHAUSTED FROM CONSTANTLY working with clients, neglecting her own inner growth and failing to prioritise self-renewal. As she approached her 50th birthday, she booked a session to see if it was time to give up her practice and find a simpler life.

"I imagined I'd be happily married by now but instead, I've been single for the past nine years. I feel invisible," she uttered wearily. Sensing that feeling unseen by others was more than a recent experience for Selena, I clairvoyantly scanned back through her childhood to see images of parents who were so self-absorbed that they made her feel inconspicuous and undervalued. They often left her alone in her room to amuse herself all evening while they lavishly entertained guests downstairs. From her late teens, Selena sought help for self-esteem issues, continuing her self-development for 30 years. It was important for me to look ahead, to identify her opportunities.

"They tell me that you've worked on yourself steadily over the years and that this effort has not been wasted," I said. "Unfortunately, you had to undo some of the tangled knots your parents tied you in before you could catch up. You're almost there now." Intuitively looking ahead, I saw a loving partner for her. "It's like you've been constructing a cake and during your final decades, you'll ice it. Your sweetest years are still ahead of you." She pondered this for a moment, releasing a long sigh. Leaning back into her chair, she glanced around the room, as though she'd just arrived. This was a brief pause after decades of relentless searching. Her expression softened and she seemed relaxed for the first time in the session. During years of forging ahead while attempting to put the past behind her, Selena had been running on fumes, unable to pause for fear of losing momentum.

My brief reminder that she had changed and evolved over the years seemed to give her permission to rest, if only for a brief moment. She had done the work through education, building a career and self-development. I was reading for her on a day when the skies seemed menacing but sometimes, towards the end of a prolonged period of endurance, there are dark moments of doubt that personal goals will ever be within reach. It's as though the darkest hour is right before a release from old patterns.

I wanted to encourage Selena to complete the self-development work she had begun. Occasionally, when someone is part-way through a healing process, it's not possible to clearly see the path ahead. It's as though so much focus has been on the past that people forget to look forward to the goals that initially motivated self-transformation. I described an introverted man ahead as a partner for her who, like Selena, was self-sufficient, kind and generous. I reminded her to complete her inner work before searching for this man so that they'd both be ready for a loving partnership when they met. By refocusing Selena on her own goals while describing a life partner ahead, it allowed her to prepare for a valuable approaching opportunity. This required her to notice how her circumstances have gradually changed and that life is already providing emotional sustenance if she is prepared to accept it.

In meditation recently, my higher self suggested that I take time every day to notice possibilities I usually overlook. I began by asking myself, "What is the opportunity for me in this situation?" When calm and relaxed, it's easier to see promise but when tired or stressed, noticing potential requires effort, persistence and detachment. It's sometimes difficult to be objective and avoid the trap of simply choosing habitual options.

I overlooked dozens of opportunities every month and realised that perhaps other individuals did as well. I began designing a clairvoyant reading to identify the energy or burdens that many of us carry that obscure vision of surrounding possibilities. When potential is hidden, we are less likely to pursue it. Although seeing promising results isn't a guarantee of success, it's an important preliminary step towards achieving personal goals. Glimpsing an outcome is essential when setting personal goals. Imagining the joy of finally accomplishing an objective can be a motivating force, especially when faced with obstacles or delays. When sailing through a storm at sea, it's important to focus on a lighthouse and not just the storm.

A specific reading examines an individual's current beliefs. It explores past incidents that have influenced the person's ability to see possibilities when faced with difficult or frustrating situations. Prospects rarely arrive with well-lit neon signs declaring 'opportunity ahead'. Instead, it is vital to deliberately look beyond obstacles to see camouflaged possibilities. At first glimpse, many paths to success appear as hard work, drudgery or risky ventures.

Being stuck behind a slow driver might actually preserve the points on my driver's licence or save my life if there's a hazard ahead. The awareness reduces my urgency to overtake the vehicle ahead. Consequently, I feel more relaxed as a result.

During a fraught business meeting, I endured 12 minutes of bellowing criticism from a person in the meeting. Had he been employed in a large organisation, he'd probably be facing some social skills training but as he worked in a small business, colleagues simply ignored his toxic behaviour. I took it as an opportunity to employ strategies that helped me to remain calm while assessing ongoing business partnership potential with that particular individual. Instead of sharpening my tongue before launching into the fray, I calmly reminded myself that this is what madness looks like. I mentally designed a T-shirt that read, 'Don't take my ranting personally' and gauged the bellower to be an XL size. Of course, I'd supply it in a hot pink or safety-vest green to telegraph the warning to co-workers. This technique helped me maintain my equilibrium during the abusive meeting.

I was grateful to have witnessed the person's instability early on, before being contractually obliged to continue working with him. Had I ignored his initial outburst I'd have felt ambushed when he fought me on every point, potentially turning my next book into something unreadable. In this instance, the opportunity involved glimpsing his irrational side before signing a contract for a book. Opportunities are not always about potential gains. Sometimes they are warnings about what to avoid.

Even setbacks can contain positive options. Before falling asleep after a busy day, I review the day while searching for missed opportunities. By listening, noticing and reviewing conversations, meetings and incidents, I can identify possibilities ordinarily overlooked. If I notice even 10 per cent more options each month, I'm more prosperous than I was the previous month.

When I can't find an opportunity in a frustrating situation, I meditate. Asking my higher self with a still mind enables me to trace the thread of events and reveal a greater image of the fabric of life. This provides a clearer vision of deeper purpose in current circumstances. With the bigger picture in mind, it becomes easier not to sweat the small stuff. In 1988, after working for several months in a psychic centre in London, I quietly decided it was time to return home to Australia. I had worked 60 hours per week for around one-third of my usual income, as the boss kept 60 per cent of all fees. Each week, without fail, he attempted to underpay me, despite the fact that I diligently recorded all of my appointments in a small diary. Readers worked from flimsy booths with dusty, threadbare carpet that had never seen a vacuum cleaner. Practitioners sat within one-and-a-half metres of each other, ensuring all predictions were heard by everyone in the room.

Without a word to anyone, during my lunch break, I walked around the cobbled lanes of Chinatown in London's West End and found a travel agent. I ventured in to book a one-way flight home to Sydney.

I asked the agent to book it as I retrieved my credit card from my backpack. This rarely used card had a zero balance on it before I left Sydney, to which I had added $2000 for the fare home. I knew it was a safe card to use. To my surprise, the agent had an issue with the card when phoning for payment authorisation. After the phone call, she explained that she'd been told that the card was stolen and was under instructions to cut it up immediately. I was still in shock when I returned to my desk empty-handed and demoralised. Arriving back at the centre, my boss glanced up and smiled triumphantly, asking, "How was lunch?" He wasn't ready to let me go, so he had energetically intervened to ensure I didn't purchase a ticket.

Initially, I was furious and frightened. How had he known what I had planned? How had he interfered with my free will? I was a long way from home and my only other credit card didn't have sufficient funds available to allow me to buy a ticket. Gradually, my mind cleared and I realised it was best not to fight with the business owner on any level, as he liked to win and had less to lose than I did. He was also a competent psychic. When I calmed down a few days later, I realised I needed to meditate and request that another experienced psychic arrive at the centre, needing a job. I also had to save as quickly as possible to purchase a flight home — in cash. Several weeks later, my boss and his wife departed for a three-week holiday in Spain. A temporary replacement reader, Christine, took their place at the centre. We quickly became friends as she didn't share the owner's agenda. Just before the boss returned, a man appeared in our doorway, asking if there were any vacant positions. Christine took his details and passed them on to the owner. After he was interviewed, I finally bought a ticket home.

Christine was a powerful channel and an excellent teacher. Our three weeks together were amazing and the highlight of my visit. I returned a few years later to study with her for six months. Reviewing this chain of events, I realised that if my boss hadn't delayed me leaving London, I'd never have returned to the UK to study with Christine nor been inspired to write a book about our spiritual experiences in the UK and Greece. Initially, I assumed that the opportunity was for me to request my replacement but actually, it was to wait long enough to find the teacher I had unknowingly travelled to Europe to meet. Several years after returning to Australia, I realised that what initially seemed like bullying and unfairness in my UK workplace was actually a carefully concealed opportunity. I eventually became grateful for the delay.

For people who struggle to find openings concealed in frustrating situations, I designed a pure clairvoyance reading to examine past incidents and life-shaping events as well as present opportunity blindness. Everyone has blind spots. For some people, these are an inability to notice personal failings whereas for others, it's a lack of awareness on how to value personal contributions to friendships or relationships. The difficulty is that it's almost impossible to know the value of something we cannot see.

Having a clairvoyant reveal some invisible influences can inspire people to discover how to do this personally. The simplicity is that it doesn't require well-developed intuition, just 10 minutes each day to reflect on frustrations that might conceal openings or paths to success. It also helps to record this information for further review later.

During this reading, I also search for gaps in knowledge that might prevent someone from pursuing a path to a goal. Trevor is an enthusiastic beginner of projects but rarely finishes anything. Consequently, he's lost two businesses, several jobs plus a recent relationship. Intuitively scouring his early life for clues, I discovered his father was the same. Trevor's primary role model had been unable to teach him how to plan a course of action to ensure he completed each important step. Trevor hadn't been shown how to map out a series of small tasks to achieve a larger goal. This deficiency had led to a life of frustration littered with many abandoned plans.

Trevor tends to launch himself into new projects without first asking, "What is the simplest way to get there from here?" or, "What steps are required to achieve this goal?" His life reflected passion without planning. He was suited to managing a team of people who completed intricate, detailed tasks while he took the big-picture approach to projects. I explained this issue to him and offered coaching on his personal goals. Over the next two months, Trevor came for weekly sessions to help him secure a new job and make a personal financial plan to reduce his overwhelming debts. Some of these steps were remedial, including washing and ironing a suitable shirt the day before a job interview, re-designing and updating his employment history, plus researching the best public transport options to ensure he was on time for each meeting.

In a few busy weeks, Trevor became the king of lists. He had a daily list, a weekly plan and a monthly outline as we began to plot a yearly map to maintain his focus. He was effectively harnessing his enthusiasm with simple planning strategies. He gradually began turning more opportunities into achievements. To offset his newly discovered discipline, he joined a group of locals to kick a ball around in the park twice a week. It was an outlet for his urge to be a reckless bulldozer and made him calm enough to continue planning.

He eventually secured a better job and commenced a new relationship. He hasn't lost his urge to forge ahead without a map or a plan but he has seen the results of self-discipline. By forming the simple, powerful habit of planning and outlining paths to his objectives, Trevor consciously overcame his initial negative training around establishing and completing goals. In just over a year, he had turned a personal weakness into a solid strength and he hasn't looked back.

NOTICING OPPORTUNITIES EXERCISE

Daily

1. Take several pauses throughout each day to ask yourself what the opportunities are for you in that moment.
2. At the end of each day, reflect and search for overlooked possibilities. Write them down on paper or on an electronic device to review them later. During these evaluations, notice any patterns.
3. It's unlikely that you'll pursue every available opportunity but it's good to be aware of choices. Each decision diminishes some possibilities and enhances others.

Weekly

1. Take 15 minutes each week to review the past seven days. Pay attention to the frustrating moments and examine them for opportunities.
2. Be aware of those possibilities you've noticed, even if you haven't pursued them.

Monthly

1. Review the lists of perceived options and decide which ones might still be worth pursuing.
2. Meditate to ask your higher self what the most significant overlooked prospect for the month was and how you can make the most of that potential.
3. Write down the main points from your meditation as a reminder for later.

It's easier to remember more when thoughts and discoveries are recorded, so it's essential to record personal insights as soon as possible. Over the years I've lost many powerful examples from client readings that, if recorded, could have benefited my tarot students. Often, at the end of a busy day, one particular person's circumstances stand out. It might provide a clear example for tarot students or readers of my next book but I have neglected to document it. Within a week, the details of a vivid example have faded and become lost.

During a pure clairvoyance reading, Samira was torn between needing a stable life on a farm with her partner and her deep desire for spiritual nourishment. She felt empty most days and the thought of fifty more years spent gazing at the same view from the kitchen window filled her with dread. What if a husband and a family was not enough and if her inner restlessness continued to grow? "If I leave now, I might regret it. Ken's a good man and he has some great ideas for the land we have," she explained. "But what if I wake up one day and I'm 50 and I've never seen the world?"

Looking ahead, I noticed she'd live in the country, raise two children and have an online spiritual group of supportive women. Three of these women lived within 200 km (not a great distance in Australian country terms) and they were likely to meet for coffee or lunch once a month. They found a few country towns that were no more than 100 minutes by car from their homes and during their meetings they swapped books, tips and discussed courses and workshops they planned to complete. This tight-knit network of like-minded people was vital to Samira. She enjoyed the social outings as well as the spiritual and emotional support. They shared books, ideas and were supportive through each other's highs and lows throughout the decades. The group grew steadily, soon numbering more than 150 members across the country and in other parts of the world.

In later life, I intuitively saw Samira travelling overseas with friends from her spiritual network, to attend courses and metaphysical development events. From writer's retreats in the Greek islands to meditation training in a castle in the Welsh countryside, they immersed themselves in short, intensive experiences, making new friends in the process. I suggested she keep a diary so that eventually, she could write a book about her travels. This might inspire others who dream of escaping the drudgery of daily life to be inspired to find their own connections to spiritual sustenance.

It was a reasonable fear for Samira that being isolated by distance and living with a man whose primary focus was growing crops to support his family, might leave her feeling spiritually empty. It didn't need to be a choice between her partner and her tribe. It was possible to have both if she accepted that many of her like-minded friends might be separated by distance.

Using the Internet, she began finding a range of online groups, then locating some members within driving distance. It was a hit-or-miss process at first until she established her own group. Gradually, she formed some rewarding friendships with women from different locations and backgrounds. These are some of the people who share her spiritual journey throughout her life. She has open invitations to stay with them whenever she is travelling and some have stayed with her when visiting Australia. She was surprised at how one European visitor was amazed to discover that her closest neighbour was actually two kilometres away. As they drove to visit another group member one morning, her friend declared, "I have never seen so much empty space. We haven't passed a single car in 30 minutes. Where is everyone?"

22. DEALING WITH DISTRACTIONS FROM SPIRITUAL PURPOSE

MANY PEOPLE ARRIVE AS NEWBORNS WITH AN AWARENESS OF their spiritual purpose for being here. However, this is often obscured beneath a surging tide of emotions, thoughts and physical demands, including desiring quality food, water, warmth, rest and regular sleep, exercise and emotional support. Without all of these needs met, people rarely thrive and spiritual purpose becomes forgotten in a weary struggle for survival.

We are spiritual beings in human form, requiring healthy physical, emotional, mental and spiritual bodies (PEMS) for life's journey. It's important to nourish these different levels to remain balanced and focused. When these four aspects align in purpose, the energies blend smoothly, resulting in health and happiness. When one or more of these is unaligned, chaos, hunger, isolation or pain emerge and there is a risk of being diverted from a deeper life purpose.

The mental energy body is easily distracted by ideas, theories, gossip, puzzles, worries, fears, stories or intrigue. In contrast, the emotional body is sidetracked by excitement, loss, regret or a deep yearning to be loved and understood. Physically, people are often distracted from purpose through the promise of excitement, pleasure, food and material comfort.

When one or more of these four aspects is undernourished, a person begins to shut down. This involves ignoring individual needs of each facet in favour of prioritising the demands of the particular system that feels starved. Essentially, the squeaky wheel gets the oil. Because the physical body generally protests the loudest, through pain, hunger or fatigue, it often demands the most attention. This usually results in awareness being drawn from the spiritual, mental and emotional needs to address urgent demands. If this becomes a habit, life can turn into a battle for physical survival. When one energy system demands all of the attention, it's easy to overlook contributing factors from the other aspects. This means that a spiritual imbalance can eventually manifest as a physical illness, as it reverberates down through the mental and emotional bodies, like the waves formed by dropping a stone into a still lake. It demands even more focus on the physical body, often to the detriment of the spiritual, mental and emotional bodies.

When our emotions crave nourishment or excitement without the mental body setting practical boundaries, our desire for passion or exhilaration can be time-consuming. Martina's overwhelming need for emotional adventure was derailing her life, keeping her unbalanced for years. When she travelled, her partner Bill was spontaneous, unpredictable and often erratic. While at home, he quickly became bored and regularly cheated on her. The downside of the excitement came when Martina fell asleep alone at night, wondering where he was and who he was sleeping with that evening. Those long, listless nights wore her out with stress, worry and fear, reducing her concentration during the day. She became exhausted, surviving on coffee and chocolate as she gradually let her friends go because she had no spare energy for socialising. Bill consumed her focus by keeping her emotionally malnourished.

Bill proposed one day over dinner in a restaurant, to the applause of fellow diners. Together they planned a spectacular wedding in Hawai'i, inviting 200 people. He wanted it to be the wedding of the year — an event his friends would talk about for decades to come. Then he abruptly cancelled the wedding and ran off with someone he met eight days before the ceremony. Shocked guests had booked tickets, flights and seaside accommodation. Martina had to apologise and repeatedly explain his abysmal behaviour.

When Martina phoned me in tears, desperate for a telephone reading, I could still clairvoyantly see them getting married in Hawai'i. I was puzzled because when the date came and went, he was nowhere to be seen.

Three months later, she phoned to tell me they were back together again. To compensate for his poor behaviour, he whisked Martina away on a quick world trip. On their way back to Australia, they stopped off in Hawai'i and married in a simple ceremony. Instead of an enormous, lavish reception, they celebrated over lunch with four friends at a noisy corner table at the Cheesecake Factory.

Not long later, Bill stormed out after a bitter argument and immediately commenced divorce proceedings. She attempted reconciliation but discovered that he had already moved into an apartment with another woman and her three children. The financial settlement turned into a battle that consumed her for the next three years. She was forced to sell her house to pay the lawyers while he craftily hid his wealth out of their reach. While she rented a cramped apartment, Bill's social media pages were filled with images of him sailing, enjoying lunch at the water's edge in Monaco and taking delivery of his new silver sports car.

Watching her dramatic life unfold was like a soap opera, only without a camera or a makeup department. I asked her during a reading one day what she imagined she might do when the divorce and settlement were over. What would she do to stave off boredom? Then I asked her what else she and her former husband might have spent their $370,000 legal fees on to have an exciting life without paying teams of lawyers, investigators and forensic accountants?

Martina suddenly resembled a shattered 15-year-old. Her thick makeup was streaked across her face and her red eyes had been rubbed raw. She wanted to cry but the tears wouldn't come. For the first time, she realised she was paying dearly for this ongoing drama. In the cold light of day, the true price of craving excitement was apparent. Legal fees and other costs swallowed up most of her final financial settlement. Even after this awful scenario, she phoned to ask if there was a chance that they might be reunited. I knew Bill would return, probably with an armful of red roses and champagne, if only to have one more dance with the girl who knew all the steps to his favourite routine. He was likely to return repeatedly, until she finally said no and closed the door in his face.

Martina seemed to be blind to the antidote to her drama addiction — peace. She believed that the opposite of excitement was boredom but this lethargy is simply a sign of disconnection from the world. Excitement's opposite is inner stillness and a profound sense of internal peace. Serenity occurs in those brief periods when people acknowledge personal needs are few and that they are profoundly content. Pausing to enjoy a magnificent view, the heady scent of fresh lavender in a garden, the sounds of soothing music or nuzzling into a pet's fur are examples of this fleeting stillness.

For decades, I've been attempting to help people locate the light and walk towards it. Sometimes this has been successful but often, my brief assistance is not enough to support them to make effective changes. When a person is living in darkness, it's very difficult to determine what is beneficial and what is simply a waste of time. Without light, judgement is impaired. This is why so many decisions lead to short-term benefits with undesirable long-term consequences. When a smoker lights a cigarette, he isn't thinking about eventual outcomes. He's stressed and believes that a cigarette will provide an immediate opportunity to breathe deeply and relax.

When people are in prolonged spiritual darkness they often barely survive — financially, emotionally, mentally and physically. They rarely have the luxury of planning long-term strategies for their best lives because they usually haven't slept well or are anxious, while living hand-to-mouth. It's not easy feeling confident when applying for a job following a night of minimal sleep or worrying about an approaching home eviction with insufficient rent money. The first impression prospective employers have is one of desperation, causing them to choose another candidate for the position.

If a healthy pot plant is placed in a dark room for several months, it grows weak, sheds leaves and eventually dies. However, if even small amounts of sunlight reach the plant, it can survive. If it subsists, the first thing it does is grow towards the light source. If it reaches the light and has sufficient water, it can flourish again.

Because daily stresses are constant and urgent for people in the dark, they sometimes learn to live with them by dissociating. They disconnect from life and from immediate circumstances to avoid becoming overwhelmed by toxic housemates, air and noise pollution, loneliness or fear. Given the choice between high anxiety and spiralling despair, they become comfortably numb. Some industries thrive by helping people to cope with the human condition. These include suppliers of alcohol, pharmaceuticals, shopping centres, online games, gambling agencies, drug dealers and sometimes even mind-numbing, repetitive work.

Dissociation is a reasonable coping mechanism for stressful circumstances but when it becomes a daily habit, it's a problem. People who use this process to disconnect repeatedly are less available for life. They exist without truly living because they are not present in each moment. Sometimes they don't remember conversations, events or even whole days as they weren't mentally and emotionally present for those periods. Not being in each moment means that they miss opportunities and warnings of impending change. This results in friendships and relationships slipping from their grasp, as they overlook signs of discontent in others.

It's easy to assess how current actions, people and circumstances provide spiritual sustenance or simply a distraction from life's difficulties, by setting aside 10 minutes a day for 30 days to begin a nourishment diary. This involves taking time daily to reflect on how people in your life in the previous 24 hours have sustained, nurtured or depleted your energy reserves. It's not about being judgemental of others but becoming aware of the influence of surrounding people and your reactions to them. It's also a chance to notice if you nourish or support your family, friends or peers when spending time together.

It's important also to consider personal habits, actions and circumstances, gauging if they nourish you, offer sustenance or deplete you. At the end of one month, look back over these dairy entries to notice patterns. Is there someone who routinely exhausts you or distracts you from deeper life purpose? Are there any daily or weekly habits that replenish your personal reserves of energy? These might include walking, gardening, writing, singing, reading, attending a book club, lunch with a friend, fishing, volunteer work, receiving a massage, a coaching session for sport, an exercise routine, chess skills, acting, painting or dance. It's basically anything that nurtures your soul or makes you feel alive and passionate about life. Sufficient nourishment leads to ongoing happiness and increased resilience when encountering obstacles.

Eating food can be physically sustaining, yet it can also provide nourishment on other levels. Grabbing a quick sandwich to eat in the car is less likely to provide the same sustenance as a warm, cosy restaurant on a cold winter's night. The venue might include a roaring open fire, the buzz of conversation from fellow diners, a choice of dishes never tasted at home and an opportunity to dress up and enjoy interesting conversations while listening to live music. Both involve eating but the shared environment includes fresh food combinations and a unique experience, such as the open fire, other patrons and the unexpected sounds of champagne corks popping as people celebrate events and milestones.

During a recent walk in a local park, I noticed a man who had developed an ingenious method for making his small dog exercise. He arrived in the park carrying the dog under one arm and a toy in the other. Placing his pet on the grass, he set a large remote-controlled car down a few metres away while the animal lounged quietly nearby. As soon as the bright orange vehicle took off across the broad expanse of lawn, so too did the dog. It leapt up from its apparent lethargy, yapping and straining to catch the toy, skidding out of control each time the car changed direction. I burst into spontaneous laughter at his brilliant solution to having an unmotivated dog. Later, I noticed a relaxed owner and an exhausted animal leaving the park. Both would sleep well that night.

Notice who replenishes your energy and who drains you. If during the month, a friend or family member depleted you once or twice, that's nothing to be concerned about. However, if someone constantly saps you at every exchange, it's time to review that relationship or even find suitable strategies for minimising contact. It's also possible to deliberately change the dynamic between you both in these interactions.

Years ago, I dropped in on a friend, Joseph, who was in the last few days of his life. A debilitating lung issue had weakened him so visits were brief, often centred around cleaning his environment, washing dishes and providing lunch and light conversation. During one of these visits, another friend was present. At first, I thought that this might make the day more fun for Joseph, until I realised that his guest, Marnie, was taking the opportunity to complain about her relationship partner, her selfish children and other personal woes.

Joseph had unwittingly become a captive audience as he couldn't leave his bed without assistance. When Marnie briefly left the room, I saw a chance to lighten the mood by saying, "And this week on *The Millionaire Complains*, we examine how to whinge to those worse off than you." Joseph smiled and winked conspiratorially. When Marnie returned, I said, "I'll take over here for today so you can go now but thanks for stopping by, Marnie." Joseph didn't have the strength to set a boundary but seeing the need, I stepped in and assisted him. He thanked me later for my intervention.

If you discover a habit that's more of a distraction than a source of nourishment, ask yourself what you might replace it with, to replenish and maintain personal energy reserves. You don't have to relinquish all diversions immediately. Instead, focus on reducing a negative behaviour pattern and develop new routines that provide greater rewards. Sometimes in summer, when my writing office heats up, I step out into another room and read a newspaper. However, a planned five-minute rest can easily become thirty minutes so instead, I changed it to a garden break. This involves filling a watering can several times and topping up the bird bath and several pot plants and watering a climbing rose. If I need further reprieve from heat throughout a day, I can water other parts of the garden. It provides a change from screen time and connection to the earth. It also allows my mind to clarify what I'm currently writing, often producing a powerful sentence to be included when I return to my computer.

Someone can nourish you on many levels during an interaction. You might feel physically sustained if you sit down to lunch in a café together, emotionally replenished through positive conversation, mentally fed through an exchange of interesting ideas and spiritually nourished by being genuinely seen and heard by this person.

Receiving respectful attention from somebody is the opposite of being shunned, belittled or avoided. A profound sense of acknowledgment from someone we love or respect can mean the difference between giving up on personal plans or believing that it's possible to accomplish them. Encouragement from a parent can inspire children to pursue goals in the same way that reassurance or praise from a friend or a colleague can motivate adults to do the same.

After a month of keeping this journal, your attention becomes more focused on who and what restores you physically, emotionally, mentally and spiritually and what depletes you. It can also help you find new people, habits and circumstances that maintain personal energy reserves. Sometimes it's not possible to change repetitive circumstances, such as a home or work environment. Instead, ensure that you are replenished outside of those surroundings to compensate for tiring or draining circumstances.

ASSESSING YOUR NOURISHMENT LEVELS

- Who, if anyone, has replenished your energy reserves in the past 24 hours? This could be through encouragement, inspiration or simply through listening without censorship.
- Who, if anyone, has depleted or distracted you from deeper sources of happiness?
- What habits or pastimes have revived your vitality in the past 24 hours?
- What activities have drained your spark in the past 24 hours?
- What new actions, routines or hobbies might provide long-term sustenance in future? Are you willing to try a different approach?

- What circumstances around you have increased your liveliness in the past week?
- What activities have drained your enthusiasm in the past seven days?
- Were any parts of you undernourished during this period?
- How can you sustain yourself going forward?

Create a summary of your observations.

Download this exercise now online at **www. paulfentonsmith.com**

23. RECOGNISING YOUR INTUITIVE STRENGTHS

POSITIVE CHOICES—AS WELL AS POOR DECISIONS, OBSTACLES faced and opportunities pursued or squandered—all reflect historical influences. Past options pursued have made us who we are. In many lives, there is often a single issue faced, mountain climbed or handicap overcome that leads to pursuing a specific intuitive direction. Someone who has developed effective strategies for a learning disability is well-positioned to teach others how to do the same. A child who has learned strategies for living with a bully can assist someone with positive techniques for similar home or workplace situations.

As professional psychics develop skills through repetition, they also sharpen expertise that shapes their personal reading styles. Individual approaches, when intuitively reading for others, prevent sessions from becoming simply predictions about possible future events. These unique styles sometimes require additional skills such as counselling, coaching or teaching effective personal cleansing.

Intuitive development students often explore a range of different possibilities, discovering innate talents in particular areas. These might include:

- Locating lost objects such as jewellery, documents or a child's toy.
- Discovering a major theme of someone's life by identifying struggles faced and strengths developed.

- Pinpointing a suitable career for someone or for the next stage of this person's life.
- Identifying individuals who have been most influential in shaping the person.
- Discerning causes of particular fears or phobias.
- Examining family burdens, passed down through the generations.
- Clarifying effective ways to remedy particular health issues.
- Illuminating destructive life patterns that hold a person back.
- Describing underlying spiritual lessons with friends, partners or family members so that the person can embrace these opportunities for growth.
- Helping people discover and value what they provide for others in friendships and love relationships.
- Exploring current spiritual or emotional burdens that can be released now, making the next steps in life lighter and easier.
- Highlighting past events and decisions that have shaped the individual.
- Describing a client's spiritual guides.
- Contacting deceased friends or relatives.
- Predicting share movements on the stock exchange.
- Identifying an individual's primary underlying life purpose.
- Revealing turning points in a person's life, such as decisions to change careers, buy a home, marry a partner, relocate overseas, pursue an investment, have a child, begin a love affair, give up alcohol, improve personal health or end a long-term friendship.

Sometimes people ask specific questions that help psychics discover their own particular strengths. When Doran arrived, he had a list of questions entirely focused on financial issues. He explained that he rarely consulted clairvoyants but that his former wife had given him my details. Doran was approaching 40 and had attempted to build wealth in a variety of ways, failing in each method. He had owned his own business for a few years, invested in a friend's business, tried a range of jobs from sales and marketing to IT and more recently, he had purchased shares with no real success. He wanted to identify the most rewarding direction to invest his time and money.

Although it was a tarot reading, I took a few moments to intuitively scan his life history. Doran was naturally a cautious, conservative investor but was taking bigger risks than he was comfortable with after a costly divorce. The way forward seemed clear. It involved taking a well-paid job and reducing his living expenses to save for residential real estate investments. I intuitively saw him pairing with a man who was already buying and renovating homes but wanted a business partner to share the costs and the decision-making. As Doran was a quick learner and eager to build his financial future, he'd be a person who adds value to a partnership.

Looking ahead for Doran, I saw them purchasing a series of properties using short-term finance and selling them as soon as the project was complete. By carefully saving all of the profits, they were able to borrow less money for each new venture. I intuitively saw that his partner financed the fifth home and kept it as his own rental property then Doran funded and kept the sixth house. After their ninth property renovation, they jointly owned the finished product, using the rental return for potential projects while mortgaging the property to reduce bank loans for future renovations.

By keeping his living expenses low, Doran was able to build wealth by not spending the profits from each completed project. Ten years ahead, I saw he was likely to own two rental properties outright, providing financial stability for his old age. Because all of his questions were focused on a single issue, it was easy to probe for more details, exploring his motivations (catching up after his expensive divorce and later feeling secure when approaching retirement) and what might work for him in the long term.

One of my specialities is looking back at decisions and events that have derailed a person before examining how the individual might return to an intended path in life. Having identified that Doran was a low-risk investor, I knew that investments in shares might be stressful for him unless they were blue chip stocks. By choosing a business partner who had previous experience with buying and renovating houses, Doran was minimising his risk. I saw his partner was practical, strategic in his thinking and didn't sweat the small stuff. He was solutions-focused and simply needed an investor to contribute money to reduce the interest paid on short-term loans. Gradually, Doran began to contribute more to each project, as he learned how to manage business deals for himself.

Looking ahead 15 years, I saw they were taking time off between renovations to enjoy weekends and social events. This usually ended when one of them noticed an opportunity that was too good to ignore. At one point, a wealthy couple who had seen their previous work hired them for a flat fee to demolish their home and manage the construction of a new one. This made them realise how they might continue to complete projects into their retirement, by hiring and supervising contractors.

Although clairvoyants often develop specialities, it's important to move beyond the narrow focus of personal preferences. Many clients are not interested in a psychic's speciality — they simply want a clear personal reading.

"I don't want to know about the past," Charlie protested as she sat down.

"Don't you want to know what has shaped you to become who you are?"

"The past is over. I can't change it. I'm here to see the future." Later in her reading, when she had accepted that she wanted a love relationship that was different from what she had previously experienced, she asked, "What do I need to change within me to be ready for a great partnership?" I paused before speaking.

"You realise that for me to answer this clearly, I'll need to examine your past, your parents, childhood and previous love associations?"

"Okay," she sighed reluctantly. The answer turned out to be simple but not easily remedied. It was important for her to begin to cherish herself as a person and to respect what she offered her potential partners. She also needed to decide early in a new relationship if her companion treasured what she provided. If not, she'd have to move on until she found someone who was capable of appreciating her.

A brief scan of her past revealed parents who didn't value themselves and were unable to appreciate the unique qualities of each of their children. Consequently, she could not see her own merit. By discovering her innate worth, she was more likely to be happier in relationships and capable of appreciating her own children when they eventually arrived. By asking what she needed to change within herself, Charlie showed she was prepared to work on herself to create a better future than her past. This is perhaps one of the best outcomes for a personal psychic reading — to depart with some homework and determination that helps shape a better future. Most people end up living with the consequences of their own choices.

Discovering a personal speciality is relatively simple. Look back on your life so far and identify one major obstacle that you've struggled with and overcome. It might be remembered as a crisis, when your world fell apart and you had to find personal strengths that you didn't know you possessed. It could have been a time when you reached for the stars and crashed to earth. Maybe the foundations of your life shattered, forcing a change in circumstances. In overcoming obstacles, you developed new strengths and abilities.

Cameron's crisis occurred before a crowd of witnesses. Having always loved to entertain people, he joined a theatre group at school. In his final year in primary school, he fought to produce a school play for the end-of-year concert. As time passed, he was too busy entertaining himself and his mates to organise rehearsals and prepare for the event. When the big night arrived, his team was completely unprepared. One team member left early to escape having to appear on stage while Cameron wished he had a valid excuse to avoid embarrassing himself. His lack of preparation was in stark contrast to the rest of the evening, which was carefully choreographed. The play was a disaster, with the audience as confused as the players. He vividly remembers being politely clapped off stage while people in the first few rows shook their heads. It scared him how badly he had blown his opportunity, especially when he had to face everyone—his family and friends—afterwards.

For the next year at his new high school, he avoided theatre groups, simply wanting to blend in. Sometimes he'd pause when passing the rehearsal hall, listening while singers and actors diligently practised their lines. Then he'd recall his own public disaster and move on. Eventually,

Cameron realised he had a choice. He could steer clear of acting for the rest of his life or be the most prepared person on the stage every time he stood before an audience. He chose the second option, over-preparing for each appearance. Maintaining a sense of professionalism has helped him to enjoy being on stage in the decades since.

In his downtime, Cameron studied the tarot, practising by giving readings to fellow actors and crew. Unconsciously, he was also honing his speciality — asking clients how prepared they were for the opportunities they desired. He developed a reputation for coaching, motivating actors to rehearse for auditions while considering every unsuccessful tryout as practice for a future successful one. Instead of the old adage that "life isn't a dress rehearsal", he believed life was a constant, ongoing preparation for a range of opportunities and that the best organised have the strongest chance of success.

As a sideline, he now coaches actors with the steps for effective auditions and screen tests. He's also in demand as a guest speaker at conferences, both for actors and business professionals who need skills for public speaking and video presentations. He explained that giving talks and teaching are still acting roles, with the bonus being that he's also the script writer. One severe public disaster was exactly what Cameron needed to strengthen his resolve. Although he initially tried to hide away from public life, a deep-seated yearning for the stage drew him back. Carefully preparing through planning and rehearsals helped to quell his fears and allowed him to thrive.

24. READING FOR YOURSELF

ONE BENEFIT OF INTUITIVE DEVELOPMENT IS BEING ABLE TO access valuable guidance when it is most needed. This helps with avoiding life's potholes or limiting the chance of making rash decisions that cast long shadows over the years ahead. However, intuitively reading for yourself is sometimes fraught with danger, unless strict boundaries are observed. It's tempting to cut corners, often with justifications like, "Oh it's just a quick reading. It won't take long." However, a hurried question asked and answered, cannot be erased when acting on incorrect information because of haste, exhaustion or even several glasses of wine.

When Graham sold his home, he banked $900,000 and made plans to buy another house further from the city. He wanted a dog, a pool and a sprawling garden. As the housing marketing was beginning to cool, he decided to rent for a while and invest his money while searching for a bargain. He scoured a range of short-term investments and landed on one that promised a return of 1.6 per cent per month. Given that his bank was offering 1.4 per cent per year, it looked almost too good to be true. He used the tarot to ask if it was a wise choice, using a one-card cut for a huge investment. One-card cuts are only suitable for simple questions. Readers use a single card for finding a suitable car wash locally, enquiring if they'll find an available table at a local café in 30 minutes, or if it is a good time to visit the gym.

As a result, he invested all of his available funds without any due diligence and later realised that his greed suppressed his instincts about the wisdom of this choice. Three months later he was carefully watching the housing market, noticing that successful home auctions in his state had dropped from 56 per cent each week to 48.2 per cent. This was good news for his next purchase but he believed it would drop even further.

The economy hit some turbulence and his investment dropped significantly. He was stuck. If he pulled his money out, it would cost him $70,000 but if he didn't, it might drop further. He waited, hoping for a rebound but it slowly dropped even more. He retrieved his cash, having lost $74,000 or around 8 per cent. Now he had to wait until homes in his price range had lost at least that much, just to break even. It took over 12 months for houses to reach that level, at which time banks had increased interest rates and tightened lending rules.

Most students agree that reading for yourself is complicated. This is because it's difficult to be objective about your own life. From our personal perspectives, we are flawless human beings who often make excellent decisions. However, the results of our choices sometimes contradict these erroneous beliefs. Most people who pursue intuitive development read for themselves occasionally. With this in mind, setting ground rules, boundaries and having a clear plan is important. Ground rules might include:

- Not reading for yourself after consuming alcohol.
- Not reading if you're rushed or uncentred by circumstances.
- Taking time to prepare clear, concise questions before beginning. It's best to type these questions out and print them for reference. It's also possible to use an electronic tablet with your written questions. Then you can write out what has been gleaned from personal intuition.
- Not reading in a public space such as at a café table, in a nightclub after meeting someone attractive or during a train journey to work where you might be distracted by people or surrounding events.
- Limiting your questions to a maximum of three or to one specific topic per day.
- If you use tools such as the tarot, taking a photo of each card layout and including the question with the image in a document file.
- Recording each session with a voice recorder on your phone or by taking notes directly after the reading for later reference.

- Limiting questions to your own life to avoid prying into the lives of others.

Essentially, it's vital that you treat personal readings with the same level of professionalism you give to paid readings from strangers. Structured intuitive processes are usually more precise and effective than haphazard psychic experiences. If you must cut corners, try to enjoy living with the consequences of hasty decisions.

TECHNIQUES FOR SELF-READING

Choose a Method for Accessing Information

- Meditation to ask your higher self specific questions.
- Tarot cards to address issues directly.
- Dreams at night through setting dream tasks and taking notes the next day.
- Meditation to access your spirit guides.
- A pendulum to guide you with yes/no questions.
- Personal instincts or hunches about your choices.

Select an Area of Interest to Focus on for the Near Future

- Career direction.
- Personal finances.
- The greater economy of your state or country.
- The effects of your current diet on your health.
- Increasing the pace of personal emotional or physical healing.
- Love relationships.
- Improving family dynamics.
- Personal spiritual development.

Over the next few months, use a preferred method to focus on a single area of interest. Regularly receive intuitive information by asking questions about that subject. After this trial period, you might feel confident to use this chosen intuitive process to ask specific questions about different subjects.

Limit your focus to one subject at first, to improve your technique with the process. Then, after a few months, expand the topics covered. First, learn to crawl before you walk, then run and finally you can dance. People who try to run before they can walk frequently receive fragmented intuitive information that might lead to poor decisions. Any fool can make bad choices. Sometimes it's difficult to live with their consequences. Occasionally, a single bad decision can cast a long shadow over a person's life. Knowing what question to ask for clarity often requires thought, persistence and patience. The results are usually worth the effort.

In a recent reading, Shirley was focused on securing a new job, having been made redundant after a company takeover. She was more stressed about turning 48 than she was about specific job areas to pursue, as she feared she might be too old to be considered to the roles she wanted. I presented a range of possible questions, explaining that she could ask any or all of them. However, some questions made others redundant. They included:

- What does the future hold for me in my career generally?
- Will I be offered a suitable new position within 10 weeks?
- Is it wise for me to apply for roles based on my previous experience?
- Is it time to change career role or industry?
- Do I need to complete further study to be more appealing to employers?
- Can I continue my education once in my next role?
- Will I find a new job through the Internet/a recruiter/a jobs app/a friend or a colleague? (Select one card for each option.)

I recommended she begin with question two as this was likely to reduce her stress about being considered too old for specific roles. The answer was 'Yes', and Shirley immediately sighed with relief.

"It's been five weeks of hell," she explained, suddenly overwhelmed with emotion. "Everyone around me is acting like life is fine and I'm quietly drowning. I could make it through another ten weeks financially but it would be great to know if I'll be offered something sooner." I instructed her to select one card while mentally asking if she'd be offered a new position within six weeks. The answer was 'Yes'. As she left after the session, she paused in the doorway and turned to say, "Thanks for this. I'll sleep well tonight — the first time in a month."

At the start of a new year, Isobel wanted to know where best to invest her marketing budget during the next 12 months. As a natural therapist who ran self-development courses, she had recently published a book. We spent a couple of coaching sessions preparing a range of options for advertising and marketing and then made several lists with questions as headings. These included:

- Which marketing avenues (from a short list she supplied) will be effective for generating new clients this year?
- When are the best months this year to use this advertising process?
- Which selling tools are likely to be most effective for increasing course students?
- When are the significant months this year to use this process?
- Which promotional options are most suitable for increasing sales of my book this year?
- When are the best months this year to publicise my business?

The first list included social media platforms, magazines, online natural therapy listings, her website, radio interviews and writing feature stories for other websites. Although Isobel was experienced with meditation, she was in a hurry, so instead of meditating daily over a few weeks or months, she asked if I could take her through the process.

Over several weekly sessions, Isobel used guided meditations where she asked each question. Once she had cut the list down to three viable options (Instagram promotions, online natural therapy listings and her own website), she asked about the best months for her efforts.

As a sole trader in business, Isobel had a limited budget, so pinpointing where to spend her scant savings for the greatest results was paramount.

We repeated the process, asking about how to increase course students and improve sales of her book. As the final session concluded, Isobel felt confident about meditation at home to ask about her next book and new courses she planned to design. It would have been quicker for her to simply book a clairvoyant reading but it was important that she ask the right questions and build confidence with her meditation skills, so that she could do it herself for the rest of her life.

One of her strongest motivations was that the previous year, she had squandered her entire advertising budget in the first four months and it was completely ineffective. She couldn't afford to splash money around without increased returns and rewards. With practice, Isobel might adapt to new marketing avenues ahead of her competitors by using her intuition and knowing the best questions to ask. She could also determine ahead of time if an interstate trip to run a course is likely to be beneficial, or if designing a product or learning a new skill might improve her business.

USING THE TAROT FOR PERSONAL PREDICTIONS

In advanced tarot courses, I usually ask for a show of hands for those who agree that it's not wise to read for yourself due to a lack of objectivity. All students' hands are raised. I request they keep their arms up if they have read for themselves in the past month. Usually, every student's arm remains vertical. People know that it's not best practice but almost everyone does it. I encourage students to make friends with each other during courses for regular practice during classes and after training sessions conclude.

If there are important questions that you need to ask with a tarot deck, the guidelines for improving accuracy when reading for yourself are:

1. When in a hurry, postpone the reading. Clear answers require a focused mind.
2. Keep the reading to one question or several questions around one topic.
3. If you ask one question, leave the cards selected facing upwards on the table so that you can revisit them over the next 24 hours. You can also take a photo of the layout for later reference.
4. If you ask more than one question or need to put the cards away afterwards, write down each question and list the answer card for that question. Then take a photo of each layout.
5. Later, open a file for those questions. List each query and include photos of the cards on the table. This minimises the tendency to overlook the whole layout while searching for a card that confirms your desires.
6. Keep thinking about the topic after you've asked your question. Sometimes a more effective query springs to mind. If so, make a new enquiry at a suitable time.
7. Review your self-readings periodically to compare predictions with outcomes. If you were wrong, revisit the layout photo and see what you overlooked. If you were right, well done — you know your card meanings. This leads to continual improvement.
8. Avoid using a one-card cut for important questions. Accuracy is diminished with a one-card cut, making it only suitable for small decisions, such as which café to eat at or when to have your car serviced. When enthusiastic beginners discover the one-card cut, they sometimes decide to ask 30+ questions in a row. This isn't a realistic prediction — at best, it's entertainment.

25. BUILDING CONFIDENCE IN YOUR INTUITION

INTUITIVE DIARY

WHEN DEVELOPING PSYCHIC SKILLS, KEEPING AN INTUITIVE diary is essential for building confidence, comparing the effectiveness of different techniques and discovering what works best for you while fine-tuning your intuition. Reading written details of accurate past predictions about your own life builds confidence in personal skills.

When Nicole realised her dreams provided correct predictive information, she enthusiastically booked a private lesson. She recalled a recent dream about her sister declaring she was expecting a new baby. Soon after Nicole's dream, her sister actually made this announcement.

I urged Nicole to keep a journal by simply writing her nocturnal visions into a book first thing each morning while the information is fresh. Over the next six months, she formed a habit of making her daily diary entries and was surprised at how much information her intuition revealed while she slept. During our sessions, I observed how her simple, grey journal was gradually being covered with stickers, glitter and an array of bright colours.

"It's all pointless information, really," she announced one day. "I don't dream about the important things like career direction, a new man or if I'll ever be able to afford a house in this town."

"Would you like a technique where you can program your nocturnal intuition to reveal information about a specific topic each night?" I enquired.

"Does this mean I could ask about my next partner and what our relationship will be like?"

"With practice, yes. It also means that you can enquire about what you need to do to be ready for a happy relationship or what you can do to progress your career." This information is freely available to everyone, especially if they train their intuition to search for it.

It's important to only ask one question or set one topic per night to avoid confusion. It's also beneficial to enquire about the same issue repeatedly until there is sufficient information. Over the next few weeks, Nicole regularly requested dreams about her next long-term partner, awakening with a range of night visions describing a man from another country (a colder climate than her own) who was in Australia to study.

She glimpsed a man with fair hair that was gradually receding. In his late twenties, he was softly spoken and shy. She dreamed about a small child with thick blonde hair who loved his pet rabbit. Almost a year after our sessions concluded, Nicole sent me an email with a photo of herself with her new partner William, who came from Canada to Australia to complete a Master's degree at university. I wrote back cheekily enquiring if there were any rabbits on the horizon yet.

Sometimes a personal intuitive journal provides a long-range record of how we arrive at the present moment. James desperately wanted a two-week enlightenment method, unaware that it's often a slow process for several reasons. "I saw a video about a guy who had a spiritual breakthrough and his whole life was different. That's what I want. Can you show me how to have that?" he asked directly.

First, transformation is difficult, especially when it requires sacrifices. These might include changing jobs, releasing friends or acquaintances who undermine spiritual development or giving up alcohol, recreational drugs and even particular foods. Second, swapping cocktail hour for a yoga mat or a meditation weekend requires some adjustments in thinking and expectations. Third, minimal effort usually results in negligible progress or minute rewards.

However, occasionally a brilliant meditation emerges, a powerful intuitive dream, a workshop that opens a new door or a book that provides a method to grow. During these periods, a diary provides an accurate record of personal progress. When experiencing momentary enlightenment or a period of grace, stillness and clarity, it's possible to make clear choices and comprehend their consequences when big decisions are required. During these fleeting hours or days, it's easier to access important information through meditation or dreams at night. Make the most of these short-lived periods and record everything in your diary. Afterwards, when life returns to normal, the tail end of these moments in light provides inner peace plus a sense of grace for days or even weeks.

In later years, a journal reminds us of how easy it is to become distracted from a path, form bad habits or allow a once-loved yoga mat to gather dust. Eventually, through revisiting this journal, it's a journey of discovery about what has worked and also which methods were unsuitable. On days when life feels bleak, reviewing your intuitive record can provide deep spiritual nourishment and remind you of what is possible from personal experience. In these moments, you're not reading about a stranger's trek up a mountain but your own personal journey. When overwhelmed by financial or emotional burdens and undesirable choices, it's good to be reminded about your skills, talents and personal resilience by browsing your own diary.

ALTERNATIVES FOR DOCUMENTING INTUITION

To keep an account of his intuitive progress, Jackson uses his mobile phone to record psychic experiences. Each brief file includes the date. Every month he uploads them to his desktop computer, where he transcribes them for quick reference. He also contemplates possible meanings and adds comments and observations in different coloured text. Jackson's intuition occurs as flashes of information, often after a phone call or a conversation with someone. Because of his hectic schedule, it's usually difficult to write anything down but he always has his phone. While walking to a meeting or in an elevator, he records what he has consciously received before it elusively slips away. Keeping a dossier allows easy retrieval of what was said, dreamed or experienced long after it has receded from the conscious mind. When reviewed, past accuracy usually builds confidence in the process while highlighting personal intuitive strengths.

Training individual intuition involves paying attention to yourself and your immediate surroundings. Keeping records helps to determine accuracy when events occur long after an intuitive experience predicted them. With increased skills and regular examinations of past intuitive experiences, you'll know what techniques work best for you and which methods are reliable in times of pressure.

ACCESSING SPIRITUAL LIGHT

Many people use psychic development in pursuit of personal growth. On a path to spiritual mastery, there are moments with flashes of inspiration or brief periods in the light, when emotional, mental and otherworldly clarity flourish. Sometimes it's as simple as a solitary dream, providing a solution to a problem.

Years ago, I was visiting Boston. A week later, after my holiday ended, I planned to teach an advanced tarot course back home in Sydney. I was pondering how I might demonstrate applying intuition to tarot readings but wanted something more engaging than simply talking about it. One night, I dreamed I was conducting a tarot workshop using a blank tarot deck. Every card contained a plain white face and yet we were giving accurate readings as a group. The next morning after breakfast, I wandered into a large bookstore, where I naturally drifted towards the mind–body–spirit section. Within five minutes, I had discovered a blank tarot deck for sale. It was the same size as a standard tarot deck, with the same blue, criss-crossed lines on the back and as soon as I held it, I remembered my dream and instinctively knew how to teach the course.

During the workshop, I requested a volunteer who asked a yes/no question. Krystal enquired if it was time for her to start a family with her partner, Ron. She had just received a promotion and wanted to enjoy her career path but Ron wanted a family immediately. She selected seven cards from a face-down tarot deck and I placed each card into position. Leaving the cards face down, I urged the students to go within and answer Krystal's question. I instructed them to write down their answers without speaking to each other.

We sat in silence for a few minutes and then I asked each student what they had written down. Every student felt that this was not the right time for Krystal to start a family. She burst into tears of relief at hearing this as she didn't feel ready for the next stage of her life. I collected the cards and placed them into the deck. One student immediately leaned forward and asked, "Wait a minute. We haven't checked what the cards said."

"That's right," I replied calmly.

"Can't we see if we were correct?"

"Okay," I said and turned over the deck to reveal all blank cards.

"What? How will we ever know?"

"You never know with certainty when a reading ends if you were correct but the fact that everyone in the room came to the same conclusion must count for something." During the next tea break, I overheard Krystal promising to post on social media when she was expecting as fellow students sent her friend requests.

That dream about a blank deck of cards was a single moment of clarity that occurred when I was asleep. Soon, however, these brief insights recede and life returns to normal. When records are kept, the notes taken on those particular lucid moments can sustain an individual during a bleak, protracted personal winter. They remind us that moments in the light can arrive unexpectedly and are often fleeting.

When writing *A Secret Door to the Universe* from 1991 to '92, I was basking in the light for long periods at a time. I was utterly focused after several months studying with my teacher in the UK. Years later, before the book was even published, I'd return to my spiral-bound notebook and read some passages. I found them emotionally and spiritually nourishing, partly because they stimulated memories of my lessons with my teacher and also reminded me of what she had been teaching me. Many years later, people told me they sometimes re-read passages from that book also, finding comfort in the pages. This surprised me. I thought it touched me because it was part of my own specific journey.

For some people, a day of spiritual light every 18 months seems like a miracle. Like golden sun peering from behind clouds on a gloomy winter's day, it's important to bask in the light in these moments. It also helps to have a few significant questions prepared for such days, to be able to ask and answer those queries with clarity. When spiritual nourishment methods become daily habits, accessing this blissful internal light begins to occur more regularly. To chart personal progress on your unique path, simply return to former pastimes. After years of meditation and pursuing a healthy lifestyle, a longed-for weekend in the pub can result in a debilitating hangover, accompanied by a profound sense of emptiness. Sometimes it's important to return to previous, self-destructive habits to be reminded that they are not as rewarding as previously imagined and that there is usually a price to pay for such indulgences. Then it's important to turn your head towards the dazzling mountain's summit and continue your personal journey out of the constant damp and shade of the valley into fresh air and sunshine.

RECORD-KEEPING PROCESS

Decide if you prefer to keep a written diary, an electronic record or a digital voice record of current intuitive experiences. Purchase a paper journal if required, or create a file named 'Intuitive Diary' on your electronic device. Begin recording personal messages, listing dreams and intuitive experiences. Place these together into a folder on a computer or in the cloud. Date every entry by making it the first thing you write or say into a voice recorder. Form this habit early to ensure accuracy.

Channel your inner librarian to cross-reference entries by name, date, event, method or location. In a saved file, it's possible to search for all 'dreams', every entry with the word 'car', 'travel' or 'job' in it. Using keywords can help when searching for a nocturnal intuitive experience about a career change amongst many entries.

Some people include sketches, symbols plus emotions experienced through dreams or meditations. This can be significant when re-reading the diary later. One diarist, Paola, explained that when she felt emotionally empty, she sketched a tomato sauce bottle in the margin of her paper diary. This was a reminder of bleak periods in her childhood, when her parents went out drinking, leaving her to feed her younger sisters. The pantry was often bare, so preparing edible meals was challenging. Some nights, all they had to eat was tomato sauce sandwiches. Her goal was to avoid 'tomato sauce days' as an adult. Spiritual nourishment for her began as sustenance through food, then gardening and eventually through a loving relationship. She has become an epic carer over the years, contributing generously to the good fortune of her children, family, friends and community.

Reviewing a personal intuitive diary provides clear proof of individual psychic strengths. It also shows gradual improvement in areas where results were initially sporadic. Don't simply decide what your strengths are based on old information. Some techniques—including tarot reading, intuitive flashes of information and psychometry—fit well with public readings, whereas others, such as dreams or meditation, are more suitable for personal development. Occasionally during sleep, I receive information about a client the night before a pure clairvoyance reading. It's as though the reading begins 12 hours before the person arrives for a session. I think this happens when I need to be well prepared for a reading with someone who is struggling in life. Occasionally, it occurs when a client is eager to begin the session and can't wait until the appointment time. If so, I mentally tell the person to settle down and wait for our agreed time.

Clients frequently phone for a reading after an event previously predicted occurs. When a person cannot immediately recognise an individual described during a clairvoyant reading, I usually move on to more relevant matters. Often in these instances, the person glimpsed intuitively hasn't yet arrived in the client's life. When the prediction occurs, clients can replay their recordings to glean what they need from the original reading. If not, they'll book another session to explore what previously seemed less important.

Keeping records of future predictions is essential to provide clarity when events unfold. It might be possible to meditate again to search for more details but sometimes, the original impression is all that's needed if you can locate your records. Another reason for making recordings for clients is that I speak quickly, telling clients what I see internally before I edit too much of it or interpret it for them. Consequently, some clients can't keep up as they don't have time to ponder what has been said. It's rare that a person understands everything revealed in a psychic reading, which is natural, especially for whole-life readings. Most individuals don't have the same needs and ambitions in their seventies that they had at age 20, so telling a twenty-year-old about their retirement is likely to seem irrelevant.

Receiving a psychic reading can be an intense experience. Many people arrive for appointments with a mixture of hopes and fears about outcomes, dreams about possibilities or even guilt about past actions. Often, clients have a particular issue in mind and focus their attention on that specific topic. Consequently, they sometimes ignore valuable information that doesn't immediately relate to their urgent questions.

When Astrid arrived for a reading recently, she explained that in her previous session, I had told her that a long-term relationship was unlikely with a man around her. Apparently, I had then described another man but she dismissed this possibility because her sole focus was Oscar. Charismatic Oscar soon faded from view when eventually, a shy, bookish man began working as an IT contractor in her office. Gradually, a friendship developed and now she was ready to ask about a possible love relationship with Will. She wasn't interested in Will during her previous reading because he wasn't in her life at the time. Instead, she focused on the man who was present.

It was my prior description of a conversation she and Will were going to have over coffee one afternoon that made her revisit her recording of the previous session for more clarity. I had clairvoyantly seen them discussing a book they had recently read where Astrid was surprised at Will's perceptive assessment of it.

Most clairvoyants record their sessions to allow clients to revisit the reading for further clarification later, as events unfold. Replaying a recording is often a positive experience as it can answer questions people hadn't necessarily thought to ask during a reading. In the past fortnight, three clients have emailed to tell me that they have listened to recordings I'd given them and each person was surprised at what they had missed on the day of the session.

Monica mentioned that she had openly scoffed at my predictions during her reading and argued with me on almost every point. I must have become frustrated with her attitude because she reminded me that I had told her when her recording arrived, she was free to delete it. In her recent email, she requested another reading and promised not to fight with me during the next session. Being naturally feisty, she did contradict me a few times during her next reading until I calmly mentioned that if she clearly knew what the future held, she wouldn't have consulted me again. She acknowledged my point with a sheepish grin and a nod.

Lucas took a more pragmatic approach to his reading, transcribing it as soon as his recording arrived. He then numbered each of my predictions or answers to questions and ticked them off as they occurred. By the time he booked his next session, he told me that he'd ticked off 19 of the 22 items. The next session with him was initially a bit stressful for me, knowing that he was likely to meticulously document my words and carefully scrutinise each point. I soon overlooked it when the reading process began and I was sifting through intuitive details in my mind's eye.

Sometimes clients are so fixated on hearing a particular answer that they ignore what is actually being said. When a psychic mentions that they won't be offered a desired promotion, they sometimes still believe that the new job will be theirs in the near future. After the position is given to someone else, a recording allows them to properly hear the actual predictions and prepare for new possibilities.

26. SIMPLE GAMES AND EXERCISES TO IMPROVE INTUITION

IT'S NOT ALWAYS POSSIBLE TO SET ASIDE EXTENDED PERIODS OF time to identify personal intuitive strengths and develop them. Instead, people are reduced to taking a few minutes to try a quick exercise sporadically throughout the day. Below is a list of games and techniques that can help to strengthen intuition and open up connections to your subconscious mind.

AWARENESS EXERCISE

This is a simple but profound centring exercise that helps to sharpen awareness within yourself and your surroundings. It can be performed at any time, either aloud or silently.

It involves simply stating, "I am aware of ..." and then completing the sentence. This is repeated 20 to 50 times with different endings. Here is one I said aloud today:

> *I am aware of the sudden brightness in my office as the sun appeared from behind the clouds.*

Other sentences included:

I am aware of a slim black pen on my desk.
I am aware of my thirst.
I am aware of the sound of a chime, indicating the arrival of a text message.
I am aware of a passenger train passing in the distance.
I am aware of the steady, repetitive ticking of the wall clock.
I am aware of the screen in front of me.
I am aware of tension in my spine.
I am aware of several birds noisily squabbling in a nearby tree.
I am aware of my feet on the wooden floor.
I am aware of the black frames of my glasses in my peripheral vision.
I am aware of a list of things to do today on my desk.

With regular attention to current surroundings, it is possible to notice threats and opportunities, with the added benefit of becoming more present in your body. Remember that possibilities for growth exist in the present moment and can be unavailable after that occasion passes. Be aware of openings at the time they appear, to swiftly seize them and enjoy their rewards. By practising this exercise, you develop an awareness of your surroundings and can extend it to important issues in your life. If you're concerned about your current job, the awareness exercise performed in the office might be like this:

I am aware of the flickering of a fluorescent light in the office.
I am aware of Kevin talking loudly on the phone in the next room.
I am aware of how uncomfortable this chair is.
I am aware of how hungry I feel, although lunch is still an hour away.
I am aware of my lack of fulfilment with my job.
I am aware of an inner restlessness to leave and find a better position.
I am aware of how lifeless the room feels despite eight people working here today.
I am aware of how often Maria sighs during the course of a day.
I am aware of looking forward to the weekly retrospective meeting we'll have after lunch.

I am aware that this meeting is a chance to be heard and to discuss ideas and results of past efforts.
I am aware of being bored with the same old tired processes.
I am aware of how we once had fresh projects every month but now new opportunities are rare.

It's possible to narrow focus towards finding more fulfilment from a current job or a new position elsewhere. This simple technique increases awareness of information that is already within and around you. The information gleaned can guide you towards better choices and previously unseen opportunities. By applying this awareness process to prospects for happiness and fulfilment, you might review each day with these questions.

Where were the opportunities for me today?
Which openings did I overlook throughout the day?
Are any of these possibilities still available to me to pursue tomorrow?
In review, what obstacles or frustrations concealed possibilities?
What options am I not seeing right now?

If you want new opportunities, change the statement to a question. The question is:

Am I making the most of what is available to me today?

By asking this question ten times a day for a month, you are training yourself to notice opportunities and to pursue some of the options available to you every day that are often overlooked.

WHAT CAN MY BODY TELL ME ABOUT THIS?

Your physical body is a valuable source of information. Discover what it can tell you about a person, a choice or a situation. By carefully and attentively sensing what your body feels, you can begin to gauge the information your instinctive or animal intuition offers.

This simple technique is especially useful for people who are quick-thinking and naturally rational in assessing situations. For these individuals, it's possible to bypass logical analysis and sense which option is best. It helps to highlight inconsistencies in an opportunity or a person, that might lead to problems later. Practise noticing your own unique body responses. Then begin to use this tool in all sorts of situations. You might be surprised to discover how often the body senses a lie or an inconsistency that the rational mind overlooks.

When driving to an unfamiliar corner of Sydney to have a desk lamp repaired, my in-car navigation system kept trying to direct me to toll roads. Taking those roads adds around $30 to the cost of the journey so I ignored it. On the return trip, I needed directions because there were lots of closed roads, dead ends and roundabouts near the repair shop so I set the sat nav for home. As I followed the directions and turned on to a main road, I sensed that the map was wrong. Within 50 metres it was contradicting itself, instructing me to turn around. I turned it off and allowed my instincts to guide me home. It was the only wrong turn I took all day.

There are many effective ways to improve personal intuition, particularly for people with high expectations who set firm goals to achieve when learning new skills. A diary is an important tool to record practice readings, the name of the person you read for and the duration of the process. It is vital to list the major points from each reading soon after concluding. It's also beneficial to follow up later to determine accuracy.

When intuitively reading for several people in quick succession, take short breaks for a cup of tea or a glass of water between each person and use this time to write notes in your diary. There is no better way to determine personal accuracy than to record the details and review it periodically. Clients or volunteers might request another session (particularly if it's free) even if your previous prediction wasn't correct, so a returning individual is not necessarily confirmation of accuracy.

Sometimes people discover greater precision for financial or job predictions than for relationship forecasts. This might highlight a possible speciality area or could suggest that more effort is required to improve weaker areas. Accuracy is often improved when a clairvoyant can give the client some background information as a point of reference. If possible, mention what a new potential partner is wearing or doing when they first meet for easier identification.

This last point seems trivial but it might be important. Many years ago, when I asked in meditation about my next long-term partner, I was shown a scene in Los Angeles where a woman walked up to me after we had spent the day apart. She had a bounce in her step and her energy radiated confidence and enthusiasm. Her face was not visible, so I immediately scanned what I could see of her to be able to recognise her when that scene occurred.

In meditation, I clearly saw her shoes. She was wearing white deck shoes with tartan criss-cross lines in red and blue across the top. That's all I saw. I had no idea why I sensed we were standing in California.

We met several months later and eventually she accompanied me to her hometown in Los Angeles. I gave a talk on the tarot while she shopped at some nearby outlet stores. Afterwards, when we met, she enthusiastically told me how much she had saved on a range of clothes and shoes. I stood transfixed, staring at her new white deck shoes, covered in thin red-and-blue tartan lines.

I assumed that the scene I had glimpsed in meditation was to be our first meeting or a situation early in our relationship, but it wasn't. In this instance, it was probably to give me time to resolve the past and prepare myself for the amazing woman who is now my wife. Relationship questions are a fundamental part of most psychic readings. If a person wants to know about his or her potential life partner, you might ask guides or your higher self the following questions.

QUESTIONS TO ASK TO CLARIFY AN IMPORTANT ISSUE

What (if anything) does my client need to resolve to prepare for a long-term partnership?
Do they currently value what they bring to their relationships?
Do they need to be reminded about their personal contribution to partnerships?
Will there be other short-term associations before their life partner arrives?
If so, what can be learned from those individuals?
Do they have more than one major love opportunity ahead of them?
If so, is it appropriate to tell them now?
Is there anything else I need to divulge about this situation today?

Although this process takes up precious time during a reading, it can also give clients valuable information about future events. The question, "Is it appropriate to tell them about this now?" from the list above is essential because the reader's task is to clarify each client's current and future circumstances without directly influencing them.

If the marriage with their long-term partner ends in divorce, it is not necessarily something to be avoided. Many people have mentioned priceless gifts they have received from relationships that didn't last, including raising loving children or discovering personal inner strengths.

One client found her career in psychiatry after a long marriage to a man who was diagnosed with bipolar disorder. After researching the symptoms and discussing available treatments with qualified professionals over the years, she decided to study and enter the field herself. She has written papers on living with a partner who is managing a disorder. I jokingly suggested to her that maybe she had finally found a way to make her former husband tax-deductible.

27. RESTORING YOURSELF BEFORE HELPING OTHERS

OCCASIONALLY, A SERIES OF DISAPPOINTING EVENTS LEAVES people feeling depleted or bereft. Although it's important to grieve losses and acknowledge setbacks, it is also necessary to reinvigorate personal passion for life afterwards. Sometimes however, a series of obstacles or losses can derail us from our paths in life.

At these times, a miracle is required. Miracles aren't always spiritual interventions or life-changing events. Sometimes they simply occur when we become aware of the beauty of life that surrounds us constantly. After the end of a love relationship many years ago, a friend invited me snorkelling one afternoon. In the cool waters off Sydney's coastline, I spent an hour swimming with schools of colourful fish at feeding time. If I remained still, sometimes they swam up to my face mask.

Ordinarily, this silent world of creatures, busily foraging for food below the surface, was invisible to me. While I floated, face down and drifting on the swell, my own issues were temporarily released. Throughout that summer, we snorkelled five days a week and every time I plunged into the cool ocean, my troubles ebbed away. Having a short break from constantly thinking about my recent loss strengthened me. When autumn arrived and the water temperatures began to dip, I felt ready to pursue my spiritual path again as the grieving eased.

Life's smaller miracles can occur when someone is briefly removed from a personal comfort zone. In an unfamiliar environment, it's possible to perceive surroundings with fresh eyes. The surprise of something new often brings people into the present moment, where recent losses or current obstacles are temporarily sidelined. In the here and now, fresh experience can add context to recent difficulties. It's like pressing a reset button. The fear or worries that consumed individual thoughts become softened by new experiences and more recent memories.

When hope is extinguished by repeated trauma or ongoing pain, it requires more persistent effort to reignite passion and optimism about the future. In extreme circumstances, a person might need the help of an outsider who can introduce sustaining patterns and habits. Sometimes ongoing weekly sessions with a therapist, a massage practitioner or an energy worker are necessary to clear residual emotions and thinking while introducing new sources of joy. It is important to regularly assess what makes you happy because what sustains a person during one period might not be nourishing later on.

Sources of enjoyment need to be simple at first, while new habits are being formed. When Lucia refused to eat any more of her stale sandwich in a park during her lunch break, she picked off a few morsels and sprinkled them on the ground for the birds watching from the safety of nearby branches. Looking back as she walked away, she saw them swoop in to feast on the remnants. The following day in the same park, they were waiting for her. A week later, she brought an array of seeds for the birds, having discovered how good it made her feel to feed them. What had begun as a short break from the office spent in bright sunshine, had evolved into a chance to support the local birdlife. Both nourished her.

Sometimes people don't need to look far for sources of joy. They only have to glance back at past hobbies and interests and notice why these were abandoned before asking if they might provide sustenance going forward. When Frank uncovered an old motorbike in the back of the garage that he'd put aside more than twenty years before, he felt overwhelmed with emotion. He had loved that rusting bike, until work demands and weekends spent restoring the house and planting a garden meant that he rarely rode it.

He considered selling it for scrap but instead chose to get quotes to restore it. While searching online for repairers, he found a few local riding clubs and gazed enviously at photos of a group of retirees who spent Sundays on country runs for long lunches beside roaring open fires. They seemed genuinely happy to be out in the elements, exploring nature while mapping out the best cafes across the state.

He emailed to enquire about joining and mentioned that he'd first need to restore his old bike. An hour later, a club member responded with a few phone numbers of reliable restorers. A few weeks later, Frank accompanied the club on a Sunday ride as a pillion passenger and was hooked. Several members asked to see his bike to assess what immediate work was required to make it roadworthy and it went from there. Frank had effectively found a new social circle with common interests; motorbikes and hearty Sunday lunches. His wife also enjoys her newfound freedom to visit galleries and explore new locations on foot with a Sunday walking group.

28. CREATING A RICH, NOURISHING LIFE

WHEN ASKED WHAT QUALITY IS MOST VALUED IN A PSYCHIC, many people consider that it's accuracy. After studying intuitive development for over 40 years, I can say with confidence that it is not precision with predictions but the ability to truly see clients. Not simply noticing the person who arrives for a reading but to glimpse and acknowledge those hidden aspects, long concealed by shame, guilt or fear of being judged by others. In some people, these parts are wounded, angry or suspicious, whereas with others, they are sensitive, creative, imaginative and kind but may have been stifled or crushed by criticism or ridicule. Being seen and accepted by another person, even a stranger, can be liberating. Sometimes this feeling is so positive that clients want to return for another reading soon after the initial session. In these instances, predictions are secondary to the simple joy of having the practitioner's full attention without judgements.

From the reader's perspective, it's easier to have more empathy and compassion for clients by tracing back into their bleak histories, discovering how they became the people they are. Often, it's possible to see that the bully was also bullied as a small child, someone who seems cold-hearted was raised by unemotional, aloof parents or a person who feels unloved and unvalued by others has not experienced being truly appreciated by people who mattered — parents. This is not to blame the caregivers because they often have their own burdens, both current and from childhood.

As adults, we live daily with our unresolved issues and occasionally, a clairvoyant reading can illuminate some of the causes for current resentments, fears and behaviours. This simple process can reignite hope within clients to evolve, resolve their pasts and choose better futures for themselves. The methods for change are not always simple or immediate. However, experienced psychics sometimes remind them how far they have come from difficult pasts and what rewards await them if they choose to continue their efforts.

NOTICING DEEPER LIFE PATTERNS

While people often arrive with immediate questions about specific issues and challenges, readers have opportunities to glimpse strangers' whole lives. Psychics can search for behaviour patterns and limiting beliefs that prevent individuals from fulfilling personal purpose. If the reader misses a person's life habits the first time, the client might return with identical questions months or years later. Then there is an opportunity to step back from surface questions, to observe deeper repetitive behaviours.

From the individual who works diligently for 40 years and barely makes a living, to someone who has never experienced a significant love relationship, life themes form when significant decisions are made and remain unchallenged. These attitudes are usually formed in childhood, often as a reaction to trauma or ongoing difficult circumstances. Sometimes people spend entire lives waiting for opportunities to arrive instead of changing outdated beliefs and negative habits that prevent worthwhile possibilities from being readily available.

When Jack arrived for his fourth reading in two years, I sensed his questions were not the purpose of his visit. He was in an unhappy marriage with three children, one of whom had special needs. Jack felt stuck. Decades of commitments, routines and family demands loomed before him like dark clouds, obscuring the horizon. In previous readings, I had explained that in six years his first child would be out of school and become more independent. In eight years, the second child would also finish school and in ten years, all of his children would be in higher education. Ten years seemed like nine years too long for him. He felt restricted by his family obligations and yearned for the freedom he took for granted in his twenties. He never imagined how many decades raising a family took, sometimes feeling trapped between work and family demands.

During this visit, he explained that he had met someone new and was considering having an affair. It's not an unusual reaction to feeling stuck or frustrated by life choices but it often only increases the hardship and sometimes ruins both relationships. I wanted to paint an opposite image of the romantic picture Jack had in his mind, so I began with a question.

"How will you cope if, in two years, you've separated from your wife and are paying your mortgage while renting a small, dingy flat with your girlfriend who is expecting her first child? Weekends are likely to be spent caring for your three children who are crammed into the tiny apartment and beginning to fight with each other because they need more space."

"It's just an affair," he argued defensively.

"Did you consider your ongoing mortgage, the two hours of travel time to work each day, the three children you currently have, the cricket practice, the support workers for your daughter and their demands on your time when you first began dating your wife?"

"Well, no."

"How will it feel in ten years if this 'short affair' becomes a marriage … and then she wants another three children?" At this point, I paused, drawing my awareness back from the immediate issue to his whole life. His mother and father had worked tirelessly to secure a stable life for Jack, who often imagined a different, somehow easier path for himself. He had accepted their preferred path of a routine job and a family, yet he wasn't nourishing himself spiritually or creatively. Perhaps while his parents diligently worked to give him a childhood unlike their own, they didn't teach him how much effort is often required to produce results. It's not unusual for caregivers to sacrifice their own needs for those of their children but sustaining themselves is paramount in the long term, both for self-preservation and to model the importance of a balanced life. Children learn by observing and tired, malnourished parents are not usually positive role models.

I realised it didn't have to be one option or the other. He was already on one path and with a bit of simple strategy, he could organise time to pursue spiritual development, plus some creative pastimes. I suggested he pick a weeknight and make room for himself. He explained that this would be virtually impossible as his daughter's support workers left at 4:30 pm each day and he needed to help with dinner, her nightly bath and bedtime routines. At this point, it was overwhelming simply listening to all of his obligations. It occurred to me that his wife, Clara, must be in the same position because she also worked full-time.

"Could you trade one evening for yourself with your wife, so that she gets her own evening free once a week too?" I asked. She also needs time for friends and creative outlets. Eventually, after discussions with his wife, Jack settled on a solution where he'd have Tuesday evenings off and she'd have Thursday evenings for herself. They agreed to vary days off if one person wanted to attend an event. After a few months, the children accepted the new routines and on evenings when his daughter, Daria, required extra assistance, they organised a support worker for evening shifts.

During Jack's subsequent readings, we explored his tendency to escape into dreams when life felt overwhelming. We discussed possible strategies for self-nourishment as his children grew up. While attempting to be a good dad to his three children, Jack had lost sight of his own needs. With both parents taking time to breathe in, to replenish personal reserves of energy and to live a bit, the whole family enjoyed the benefits. Since then, Jack has joined a meditation group and eventually became a meditation teacher, while Clara resumed her music studies, abandoned when Daria was born. Both of them appreciated the time spent away from the family and felt more rejuvenated when they were together. This arrangement works well but will evolve over time as the children become more independent and need more transport options for after-school sports and activities.

HELPING PEOPLE DISCOVER PERSONAL STRENGTHS

Sometimes clairvoyants need to be counsellors, coaches or to ask clients strategic questions to help clarify their options. Occasionally, people want help to make maps towards desired goals. When this happens, they might return periodically to refresh these plans and explore current challenges and opportunities.

These are times when it's important for the reader to highlight the opportunities contained within challenges, turmoil or change. An unexpected retrenchment from a steady job, a sudden separation or an unplanned addition to the family can all increase stress levels and a sense of dread about the future. When this happens, clairvoyants can look ahead to better times and reassure people that the current upheaval will pass.

When Dianne felt overwhelmed during a reading, she looked at me and said, "It's been so hard for so long. I just want a life where the sun always shines and it never rains."

"I understand that your burden feels unending. You're weary from all the effort required but be careful what you ask for. You have just described a desert." She laughed at this, so I took the concept further.

"It sounds like you want less Seattle, Washington and more Phoenix, Arizona as a life climate. Does that sound right?'

"No. I want Hawai'i, Barbados or Nice in France."

"I'll tell the chef and see what he can do. Perhaps instead, we can examine the ingredients of the life you already have and see what we can make from those." We both paused for a few moments to consider this idea. Skills, talents and personal strengths are all elements from which we can create rich lives.

Sometimes people overlook learned skills or innate talents that can propel them forward. New strengths can be honed and abilities refined until they open unique paths for income, happiness or moments of joy. Knowing your personal strengths can mean the difference between a life of endless struggles or thriving. Recognising the ingredients that you have within for a positive life is the first step towards creating that experience.

If this seems too difficult, find someone who can coach you towards acquiring the skills necessary to climb your personal mountains in life. Sometimes it's necessary to practise with smaller goals before tackling serious, life-changing objectives. Continuing the cooking analogy, it's best to begin with making pancakes before tackling a soufflé.

29. SPIRITUAL NOURISHMENT FOR YOUR LIFE JOURNEY

WITH INCREASING RATES OF ANXIETY, DEPRESSION AND STRESS, many people seem unaware of deeper human purpose. Having effective, simple methods to remain unruffled by life's chaos are essential to ongoing inner peace. Just as elite athletes need to remain mentally centred and focused on their long-term goals, it's also important to have a personal lighthouse or point of motivation for ongoing, deeper development. This ensures spiritual progress throughout life. The rewards for effort are gradual but measurable, not awaiting each individual in the afterlife. They include less stress, anxiety or anger when confronted with obstacles, as we are capable of looking beyond immediate frustrations to identify opportunities for personal growth, change and happiness. The huge amounts of energy expended with anxiety, stress or frustration can be devoted to meaningful, sustainable pursuits.

Spiritual awakening involves weaning ourselves from short-term distractions and concentrating on profound nourishment. Although diversions and supportive activities outwardly look the same, they are as different as a sugary snack and a wholesome meal. It's instant gratification versus ongoing sustainability.

Activities That Can Provide Nourishment:

Physically: Exercise, games, walking, gardening, yoga, receiving a massage, swimming, dance, movement, mowing a lawn or constructing a beach house, swimming, surfing, cycling, hiking or hang-gliding. Sports, gym sessions or judo classes also provide physical replenishment.

Emotionally: Being with friends, painting, writing, playing a musical instrument, singing, gardening, swimming or spending time with pets. Enjoying time alone to reflect can also be intensely rewarding.

Mentally: Studying, reading uplifting books, attending inspiring talks, yoga, meaningful conversations, discovering new concepts and ideas. Taking time out regularly to carefully consider different life theories and perspectives can be mentally refreshing.

Spiritually: Volunteering, prayer, meditation, regular periods of reflection, yoga, time spent surrounded by nature, painting, music, poetry, helping others to find purposeful pursuits in life or through reading inspirational books. Contemplating encouraging words or being of service to others can also help.

As more people withdraw from established religions, many are unable to find suitable alternative spiritual sources of nourishment. Instead, happiness becomes the new fulfilment. Big business loves this because striving to be content is a short-term goal. It soon loses its lustre. The new shoes purchased weeks ago no longer have the same allure they once held. By distracting ourselves with new trinkets, we are briefly unaware of the underlying hunger for something more meaningful. When we remain spiritually undernourished, distractions can dampen any awareness of more meaningful pursuits.

When beginning to nurture ourselves spiritually, people initially notice how exhausting life becomes without work/life balance. Spending extended time in an office, in traffic or reading newspapers tends to deplete us. For a sensitive person, watching the news is often a depressing experience. An antidote to this is to meditate more, especially if this includes drawing down light and personal cleansing. An effective period of reflection leaves people feeling centred, calm and focused. When you're present in the moment, creative ideas and solutions to problems flow more easily. Focused people are usually available for immediate opportunities. They're often also more effective with less effort for hours after a relaxing meditation. When unburdened by anxieties and worries, it's easier to contemplate possibilities. It's also much more enjoyable.

During a recent yoga session in a local community centre, I noted that the large, well-lit room had twin doors that opened to a glorious vista. There was a deep veranda that would be suitable for students to eat lunch during daytime courses. The room had seating for 50 people stacked against one wall and was air-conditioned, a necessity in Sydney summers. After class, I asked the teacher if the venue was usually booked on weekends and he said that most people wanted it for weekday use. I had found my next course venue, 10 minutes-drive from home.

When Lara asked about her career direction, I intuitively saw her working for a medical supplies company. Her job involved contacting hospital staff to showcase her company's products. She was one of four people in the organisation who shared territories across the state. Although Lara was trained by the company to email potential customers, she realised that this was a wasted effort because they were very busy people. Instead, she phoned and invited them to lunch. She followed each call with an email that included three possible lunch venues with links to their menus. During an initial lunch, she was charming, flattering and keen to encourage them to talk about themselves. Afterwards, she handed them a folder of information about her products.

Lara then followed up with a second lunch invitation several weeks later, with three new possible venues. During the second lunch, she mentioned her products briefly between courses and glasses of wine. Soon, her manager was asking her to justify her expenses, as the lunch receipts steadily increased. She asked him to take the longer view, as she was acquiring customers who might use their products for years.

During one of her lunches, she was amazed at a grilled fish dish with a citrus flavour. Being a person who was constantly on the lookout for opportunities, she explored the possibility of signing up a different client. After lunch, when her guest had departed, she ventured into the kitchen to speak with the chef. Lara explained how she enjoyed her dish hugely and that it was a unique experience. She asked him what the unusual citrus flavour was in that recipe but he coyly avoided answering her. She enquired if he'd be interested in her finding a top-quality company to produce his food for freezers in an exclusive range for supermarkets. He agreed to consider the idea and she left with a challenge to find a suitable supplier. If she was successful, she'd receive an ongoing percentage of the profits and it might be the first of several chefs she could manage. This arose out of her ability to notice possibilities around her while taking a potential customer to lunch.

Anyone can learn to do this. It only requires that they are in the present moment and prepared to sift through those ideas that won't work, to find those that will. Several years ago, I resolved to notice 10 per cent more opportunities per year. I don't need to pursue them all — simply notice them and choose from life's menu.

Drawing down spiritual light in contemplation involves releasing daily demands, calming the mind and then requesting light and grace to fill your body. This illumination usually pours down through the crown (top of the head) and flows steadily throughout the physique, cleansing and restoring the physical and emotional bodies. With practice, it's a simple, rewarding activity. As the light exits through the feet, it sweeps away tension and negativity, leaving a person feeling tranquil, centred and still, like a peaceful, calm day in a sunny park. This process is physically cleansing, while restoring personal reserves of spiritual energy.

For people who find contemplation difficult, a guided meditation download helps. White noise or sounds of waves lapping at the shore can also be calming, especially for auditory people, who are easily distracted by surrounding conversations or jarring sounds. Sometimes the process is more effective when someone acts as a guide, keeping the meditation on track. For experienced meditators who want to immerse themselves in a deeper, more powerful process, guided group sessions can help. Meditating in a team of people familiar with the procedure is like taking off from an airport runway. More adept people take everyone else with them.

For many years, I struggled with meditation, suffering from a wandering mind and nomadic eye. Every sound aroused my curiosity and set me thinking about what might be happening in the next room, street or suburb. This was dramatically reduced when I learned to cut psychic energy cords connecting me to others before deepening my focus and concentration. Finally, I was able to reach profound depths, with a still mind and body. Then, gradually I noticed that intuitive information available to me was clearer and more relevant to my immediate issues. What felt like a few minutes was often half an hour or more as I asked questions and listened carefully.

Psychic energy cords are invisible threads linking people to each other. They are natural energy streams of connection that flow between individuals. The more cords a person has to others, the less centred this individual is when attempting to meditate. It's like trying to find a peaceful moment when all of your friends and family are visiting at once. You're surrounded by laughter, conversation, disagreements and unspoken undercurrents. Just when you find a quiet spot to reflect, everyone wants your attention. Cutting these cords is effectively like turning off your phone, drawing the curtains and briefly disconnecting from the demands of everyday life. It provides a moment of calm, to breathe deeply and replenish personal reserves. Then meditation becomes a great reward, an opportunity to remember your spiritual self and fundamental life purpose. Meditation can be addictive, especially when it provides a reset button on stress and the urgency of everyday life. It makes a busy life more effective because people can drop the associated stress with each meditation. They can also pause to reflect, allowing for better solutions to current demands.

If contemplation is difficult, try spending a weekend away alone in the country. Out of sight, earshot and hopefully out of phone range, it's possible to be less distracted during meditation. Sometimes there are persistent cords to people from the past. Occasionally, interference comes from longstanding connections to former partners, work colleagues or deceased parents, especially if there are unresolved issues with particular people. These tenacious cords require karma to be resolved before being severed. Because of unfinished history, it's not always possible to eliminate all cords. However, cutting most of the links vastly improves concentration for meditation and for life.

In courses, I demonstrate how the demands of others can reduce the self-focus required to meditate. Using two volunteers, we role-play to bring the theory to life. One volunteer describes two people in their life that are currently distracting or emotionally needy. The other participant and I momentarily become those people, asking questions, talking for the sake of it or even wailing to get attention. It's immediately apparent that our noisy interruptions are ruining their focus.

Setting up a few simple, nourishing daily routines is like insulation from craziness and unreasonable expectations. These might need to be varied with the seasons, as an extended daily walk is not possible during a snowstorm, whereas swimming on a hot day is positively invigorating.

SIMPLE DAILY ROUTINES FOR NOURISHMENT

- Reading an uplifting book.
- Helping someone who needs support, such as an elderly neighbour or a friend.
- Fifteen minutes of gardening or a short stroll in nature.
- Playing a musical instrument.
- Time spent with a colouring-in book or paints.
- Using a guided meditation or simply reflecting silently alone.
- A conversation with a friend.
- Taking time to be consciously gentle with yourself and others. Kindness is like love in that it softens the way ahead in life for everyone.
- Listening to a positive podcast.
- Developing good sleep routines.
- Thirty minutes spent cleaning or improving your environment.
- Half an hour of yoga practice.
- A walk with the dog.
- Swimming in a pool, in the ocean, a lake, river or a dam.
- Fifteen minutes spent watering or pruning the garden.
- Listening to uplifting music.

- Watching a comedy.
- Physical activity such as walking, jogging, roller-blading, yoga, dancing, tai chi, judo lessons, swimming, stretching, vacuuming or climbing a rope.
- Regular gym workouts.
- Keeping a gratitude diary.
- Singing along to a favourite song.
- Mowing a neighbour's lawn.

As bizarre as it seems, I find cleaning leaves from a swimming pool a zen-like practice. The gentle movement of the pole and the swish of the net culminate in a satisfying moment when I can stand back and briefly glimpse the pristine water. It doesn't remain clean but that's not the point. There is a forest of tall gum trees over the fence in the neighbouring park ready to deposit fresh loads of leaves with every breeze, which means it is necessary to repeat this process in a day or two. As I gaze into a sparkling clean pool, I've momentarily restored order to my private corner of the world. It's a satisfying feeling until I notice a single leaf gracefully drifting towards the shimmering water. It's a tranquil reminder that sometimes perfection is fleeting.

When nourishment is most required, ideas and inspiration are often scarce. Making a plan ensures being prepared when suddenly overwhelmed or unable to imagine what you can do to replenish your soul. A comprehensive list includes self-nurturing activities for each season, daytime or evening, alone or with others, as well as simple practices for use when exhausted or during periods of prolonged stress. Reach for the list of positive daily activities when bereft of ideas of how to replenish yourself and get ready for action.

Positive habits insulate people from some of the surrounding stresses. In the 21st century, it's possible to have information from around the globe at your fingertips, but not much of that is helpful and most of it is not essential for wellbeing. How often does news from afar (wars, extreme weather events or financial crises) negatively affect your equilibrium? Instead of avoiding the world to prolong inner harmony, it's easy enough to reset yourself when necessary.

Restoring inner peace ensures that you don't remain uncentred for hours or days after upsetting events, making poor decisions during these worrying periods. One of the core benefits of recentring is having the choice to shake off stress, anxiety or fear. By consciously restoring inner harmony after periods of tension or chaos, you gradually build resilience. This ensures that you remain on a positive path despite what life hurls at you. Remembering to reach for techniques to release stress or centre yourself requires practice, until it becomes another unconscious positive habit. This might mean taking the dog for a long walk after work to reconnect with nature and release the stress of a working day. This helps with sleep at night and ensures that the dross resulting from daily frustrations isn't offloaded at home every day.

Each rewarding decision stimulates new potential options, especially for people who take time to notice choices that might be easily missed. With clear awareness of potential openings for growth and progress, the start of each day becomes a quest or a challenge to discover what possibilities the day holds. The end of each day provides a chance to look back, to discover even more choices than you originally noticed. When you begin to identify them, possibilities suddenly seem to be everywhere.

It's a heady experience, contemplating the rewards that might follow a successful outcome of a plan. Reliable intuitive practices are extremely helpful with wise decision-making. Successful lives might involve some luck but they usually include careful choices. Awakening your intuition is a process of adding valuable skills to decision-making, so that moments of lucky coincidence are followed by positive choices. The combination of being on the lookout for opportunities, building skills to prepare for fortunate breaks and using intuition to make better choices reduces restrictions that limit many people from fulfilling their potential. In harnessing personal intuition to make better choices, a person can save that most valuable resource — time. With a clearer view of opportunities and better use of time, the impossible is sometimes within grasp. What are you reaching for?

GLOSSARY

ANIMAL INTUITION

This involves an instinctive intuition or inner awareness that is survival-oriented. It's often used by animals to avoid predators and survive threats to life. In humans, it can surface as gut feelings, hunches or areas of the body that tighten up when a person is not consciously aware of an impending threat.

ASTRAL BODY

Humans comprise several forms that range from dense (the physical aspect) to very fine energies, such as spiritual facets. The astral body is finer than the physical and emotional forms. It can travel without the physical being, usually when an individual sleeps at night.

ASTRAL TRAVEL

This occurs when the astral body (a fine energy body) leaves the physical body, often during sleep at night. These brief sojourns might involve visiting a friend or a family member, stepping out of the body to farewell a friend who has recently passed away or exploring foreign cities or favourite locations. With patience and practice, it's possible to consciously astral travel while awake. The benefit is that you can remember what you experience when roving.

AUDITORY

Auditory psychics have keenly developed hearing, particularly for listening for internal assistance from spiritual guides of the higher self. During professional readings, auditory readers might say, "I'm being told that your late husband loved to ride his motorbike every Sunday," or, "I was given the name Michelle. Does this mean anything to you? I'm being told that Michelle misses you dearly."

CLAIRVOYANCE

This is from the French word for 'perceptiveness'. It is seeing beyond the immediate physical environment to events in the future. Beginners who initially experience clairvoyance often want to see just how far they can see into the future. This is not recommended, as they frequently see beyond their own existence. Being reminded that life is temporary can be overwhelming.

HIGHER SELF

The spiritually evolved part of each person. This aspect of each individual has the long-term vision required to act as a guide, a wise friend or a spiritual sherpa in life quests.

KARMA

Karma is a Sanskrit word for a deed, action or choice and its consequences. In life, people sometimes pursue goals with little concern for unintended consequences. However, in the wider view of life, many individuals are forced to endure unexpected costs or burdens for past personal choices and actions. The purpose of karma is to help people understand how their actions affect others.

KARMIC CORD

A psychic energy cord (see 'Psychic cord') results from karma formed between two people. Only when the karma is resolved can this cord be dissolved. If two people were in love and their relationship ended in betrayal, that pain caused to the aggrieved person must be felt and understood by the other partner before that cord can be severed. Often, with an understanding of pain comes the desire for atonement, as a way to settle the emotional debt.

KINAESTHETIC

Kinaesthetic intuition combines animal intuition with psychometry (see 'Psychometry') to sense information about others. These sensations are usually physical, such as bodily feelings, tastes, smells or emotions and don't arrive as images or sounds.

MASTER

See 'Spiritual master'.

MEDITATION

Meditation is a process to still the mind in order to hear the deeper, more spiritual aspects within. Meditation for spiritual development sometimes involves giving the conscious mind a repetitive task, such as chanting or breathing rhythmically, to briefly bypass thinking processes. It occurs naturally when a person swims 20 to 30 laps of a pool, jogs for 40 minutes or engages in any routine task that allows the mind to settle. This can include knitting or folding freshly washed clothes.

MENTOR

Someone who has direct personal experience of having done it before. They can say, "This worked for me and it might work for you."

PSYCHE

The soul or spirit, often mirrored through the mind.

PSYCHIC CORD

An invisible cord of energy, usually formed by desire, that links people to friends, family members, partners — present and past. These energy cords are unconsciously used to distract people from life's intended purpose, especially when family members or friends want you to behave in certain ways that support their own agendas.

PSYCHOMETRY

A process of sensing residual energies left in objects by owners or people who regularly handle them. It's possible to form a psychic cord from the object to the owner and intuitively 'read' the owner's life. One weakness of this method is that if an individual has physical health issues, the intuitive reader or psychometrist is likely to feel those symptoms inside his or her own body.

SLEEPER'S CLASS

Sometimes when people fall asleep at night, the spirit body (which doesn't need slumber) leaves that physical location and finds a spiritual teacher for a sleeper's class. For brief periods during nighttime rest, a range of different spirits might attend study groups to further personal spiritual development. These group experiences are usually forgotten upon awakening.

SOUL

The soul or psyche is the finer, energetic essence within each individual. This spiritual aspect doesn't require food or sleep at night, but it does need regular nourishment to thrive. Soul sustenance can include regular meditation, prayer, creative activities, service, helping other people or remembering God or the source of spirit from which we are all derived. The soul inhabits and animates the physical body but separates from it at death.

SPIRIT

Another term for soul (see 'Soul'). A spiritual person is someone who acknowledges the soul and nourishes it for the journey through life and beyond.

SPIRITUAL GUIDE

A spirit of a deceased relative or an unknown individual who is between lives, who can provide information and guidance through dreams or meditation.

SPIRITUAL INTUITION

An inner awareness that allows people to glimpse likely outcomes of current choices and underlying lessons or deeper purpose in current circumstances. It can also be used to contact spiritual guides, your higher self or ascended masters for personal development, learning or comfort when exhausted with the trials of life. Awakening this type of intuition is also known as opening the third eye.

SPIRITUAL MASTER

A person who is spiritually adept. This is someone who understands the consequences of everyday choices, is aware of personal karma and has various methods for individual spiritual nourishment. His or her focus is both in this physical world and the hidden, spiritual worlds.

TEACHER

This is an expert in the field who can show others skills to achieve desired outcomes. An effective teacher usually has a range of methods for spiritual development and can train other people in the required methods, including meditation, inner sensing, listening to the body or setting dream goals at night. Experienced educators can identify if students are kinaesthetic, auditory or visual by nature and guide them towards strengthening their natural talents.

VISUAL

Image-focused psychics are clairvoyants — clear-seeing. They can inwardly glimpse scenes of the future. When clients ask about a new home or where they'll retire to, these individuals can describe the building, surrounding gardens and identifying objects, as they see them in their mind's eye. It's the same way we recall past experiences. This helps clients to recognise the property or event when first glimpsing it. Image-focused intuition might provide clear internal pictures of the back garden, the fading wooden garage and a rickety gate joining a winding path leading to a sheltered cove containing the remnants of a shipwreck at low tide.

ABOUT THE AUTHOR

COUNSELLOR AND CLAIRVOYANT, PAUL FENTON-SMITH IS THE author of 13 books on personal development. His passion and enthusiasm for his work make him popular on television and as a guest speaker and teacher.

After completing palmistry studies in Adelaide in 1978, Paul moved to Sydney in 1980 and studied tarot reading in 1984. While honing his skills in private practice, he founded the Academy of Psychic Sciences in 1985 to teach palmistry and tarot reading, adding psychic development some years later.

Paul received a Diploma of Clinical Hypnotherapy in 1986, studied counselling in 1992 and received a GradDip in Counselling in 2016 (Western Sydney University). He also studied meditation and intuitive development techniques in the UK in 1991.

Aside from his teaching commitments at the Academy, Paul works in private practice in Sydney as a clairvoyant, counsellor and hypnotherapist and conducts courses internationally. Through practising and teaching intuitive studies for more than 40 years, Paul encourages his clients and students to accept only what they can see or experience for themselves. He believes that everyone has intuitive talents and passionately encourages people to explore these areas in practical ways.

Books

The Tarot Revealed (1995/2008)
Astrology Revealed (1997)
A Secret Door to the Universe (2017)
Mastering the Tarot (2000)
Finding Your Soul Mate (2001/10)
True North (2002)
Palmistry Revealed (1996/2017)
12 Paths to Fulfilment (2003/14)
Tarot Masterclass (2007)
Intuition (2011)
Advanced Tarot (2021)
Activate Your Psychic Ability (2024)

www.paulfentonsmith.com

ACTIVATE YOUR PSYCHIC ABILITY

The Power of Intuition Revealed

PAUL FENTON-SMITH

The smallest of choices can change the course of your life. Your psychic senses are your keys to creating your best path forward.

When you learn to look ahead, your insight will save time, energy and heartache — steering you towards worthwhile goals and deeper purpose. Activate your natural psychic ability to build faith in your instincts and be true to the outcomes of your choosing. This thorough and practical how-to includes approaches, strategies, exercises, activities, quizzes, anecdotes and expert advice to help you:

- Identify your psychic strengths and connect with your internal guidance.
- Measure the accuracy of your intuitive impressions.
- Know which questions to ask for the most revealing answers.
- Enhance your relationships with people and animals in the physical and spiritual realms.
- Become aware of potential opportunities and discover how to harness them.

Gain awareness of where the choices, connections and actions of today will take you so you can greet every pivotal moment of your life with greater wisdom, calm, confidence and clarity. Why leave your destiny to chance?

240 pages, paperback
ISBN: 978-1-922573-91-9

ADVANCED TAROT

An In-depth Guide to Practical & Intuitive Tarot Reading

PAUL FENTON-SMITH

This in-depth study of the tarot explores the symbolism, meanings and interpretation of all 78 cards of the tarot alongside anecdotes and insights drawn from decades of reading and teaching experience.

Enhance your knowledge of traditional meanings with intuitive impressions for clear, supportive and insightful readings. Understand the reading process, word questions for more accurate readings and answer Yes/No questions with confidence.

This comprehensive 556-page exploration of the tarot includes tips on reading under pressure, setting boundaries, distant readings and cleansing between clients.

- Upright and reversed meanings for general, career, relationship and health questions for every single card
- Essential questions menu
- Range of go-to layouts
- Sample interpretations
- Quick reference charts and correspondences
- Full-colour images from the *Rider–Waite Tarot*

A one-stop resource for tarot newbies and those wanting to take their readings to a professional level. Renowned author and teacher, Paul Fenton-Smith has over 40 years' experience and is the founder of the Academy of Psychic Sciences in Sydney. Whether reading for clients, teaching or conveying his knowledge through his books, Paul's insightful and practical approach brings clear benefits to people's everyday lives.

556 pages, paperback
ISBN: 978-0-648746-82-9

NOTES